POWER UP!
OUTDOORS
EDITION

DEVOTIONAL THOUGHTS FOR SPORTSMEN

DAVE BRANON, EDITOR

Discovery House.

Discovery House is affiliated with Our Daily Bread Ministries,
Grand Rapids, Michigan.

Requests for permission to quote from this book should be directed to:
Permissions Department, Discovery House, P.O. Box 3566, Grand Rapids,
MI 49501.

Unless otherwise indicated, all Scripture quotations are from the *Holy Bible,
New International Version*®. NIV®. Copyright ©1973, 1978, 1984 by International Bible Society. Used by permission of Zondervan. All rights reserved.

Interior design by Sherri L. Hoffman

ISBN: 978-1-62707-471-1

Printed in the United States of America

First printing of paperback edition in 2015

POWER UP!

OUTDOORS
EDITION

CONTENTS

INTRODUCTION

The Outdoor edition of the *Power Up!* devotional book series has a distinction that none of the other volumes in this series can have. Only this version can claim to have its activities mentioned in Scripture. There is no baseball in the Bible (sorry, "In the Big Inning" does not count) and there is no golf in the Bible—but there are hunters (Nimrod; Genesis 10:9) and fishermen (Andrew and Peter; Matthew 4:18–20).

Indeed, as you read through the articles in this book, you will notice that several of the writers refer to the fishing analogy Jesus used in the Matthew 4 passage as He described to His men the concept of "fishing for men."

Men and women who take up fishing and hunting as recreational activities have another advantage. They have the grand opportunity to step out into God's created world and enjoy His majestic ability to build beauty into the landscape of this world His hands have made.

And they have the opportunity to practice careful dominion of His creation.

Those who love the Lord and enjoy recreational hunting and fishing have a responsibility to treat the creatures they encounter properly. That's why careful hunters only harvest animals that are being hunted within the bounds of responsible management. For instance, in some states it is an essential part of wildlife management for certain numbers of animals to be taken each year lest their numbers overwhelm their habitat. Without proper controls, animals would starve throughout a region.

In one mid-sized city, for example, a nature preserve had to cull a number of deer from its land in 2008 to ensure balance.

Likewise, responsible fishing includes practicing catch-and-release tactics whenever feasible to avoid depleting fish populations.

In this book, fishing and hunting stories provide outdoorsmen and outdoorswomen with interesting jumping-off points to help them understand vital biblical teaching. The fishing-hunting aspects of the pages are secondary to the presentation of life-changing truth from the Bible. The most important element of each page, then, is the opportunity to explore Scripture and to seek new ways to live in a growing relationship with Jesus Christ.

People who fish and hunt have learned the important lessons of the pursuit—keen observation and careful action. It is our hope that as you observe the truths in this book and as you put them into action in your life you will grow closer to the God who has created for us such a magnificent world of nature.

DAVE BRANON, EDITOR

THE TOP 100 HUNTING AND FISHING TIPS

Be careful."

That probably should be the No. 1 tip any hunter or fisherman should pay attention to. It can be dangerous out there as you stalk your prey or dip your line in the water.

But if you are a true camo-wearing, shotgun-toting hunter or an authentic worm-baiting, tacklebox-carrying fisherperson, you are probably looking for more practical help. You probably want to know how to make a good mock scrape or how to snag a hungry walleye.

We've got some of that kind of help for you in the Top 100 Tips at the end of each devotional article in this book.

We've divided the tips into categories: hunting, hunting safety, fishing, ice fishing, and several others. That way, you'll be able to leaf through and look for the kind of tips you most prefer.

These tips come from some guys who have spent a lot of time wetting lines and firing guns.

Jeff Olson, who in real life is a biblical counselor for Our Daily Bread Ministries, doubles as a pretty good outdoorsman. He has fished for salmon in Alaska, fly-fished for trout in Utah, and hunted deer in Michigan.

Tracy Breen has created a career for himself out of hunting and then telling people about it.

Maury De Young loves the outdoors so much that he created a ministry to share what he knows with others. Formerly a pastor, Maury now tries to get more and more people out into the fields and streams through his outreach called Sportspersons Ministries International.

Combined, these three have logged thousands of hours under God's sky trying out lures, experimenting with the best ways to use treestands, and studying the habits of multiple species of fish, fowl, and four-footed friends. So they know what it takes to be safe, to get the game, to not get lost, and to accomplish the dozens of tasks it takes to be a successful outdoorsman.

Best wishes as you incorporate their wisdom into your own adventures in fishing and hunting.

—DAVE BRANON

POWER UP!

OUTDOORS
EDITION

1. WHAT'S IN A NAME?

"Jesus looked at him and said, . . . 'You will be called Cephas' (which, when translated, is Peter)."

JOHN 1:42

Fishing enthusiasts. I know you exist. Admit it. You love the thrill of a perfect cast, a bent pole, and pulling in the "big one."

You are in good company. Yes, it's true that Jesus didn't actually wet a line, at least not that we know of. But He did hang out with a group of fishermen. One, in particular, was quite a character. He was impulsive, outspoken, and unpredictable. Most of us know him as Peter. But before he met Jesus, he went by the name of Simon.

FAST FACT:

A true fishing enthusiast knows that there are more important things in life than fishing—but he or she just ignores those things.

When Jesus first saw him, He changed his name to Peter, which meant "a rock" (John 1:42). Why did Jesus mess with his name? In biblical times, it was frequently hoped that a person would take on the meaning of his or her name. Peter wasn't a rock of a person when he first met Jesus. But Jesus didn't merely see him for who he was—a hotheaded choleric who would tuck his tail in and run when the chips were down. He also saw him for who he could be—a rock, a trusted follower He could count on.

Are there things about you that you wish were different? Maybe even your name?

Perhaps deep down inside you wish you were less angry and more patient? Maybe you wish you were less afraid of what others think and more courageous to stand up for what you believe. Changing your name won't help, but changing your outlook will.

Remember that Jesus looks at you the way He looked at Simon Peter. He sees both who you are and who you could be for others and for God. And He will help you become the person He wants you to be.

—JEFF OLSON

FOLLOW THE COMPASS

Name some aspect of your character that you would like to see changed and begin to pray for God's help to make you change.

From the Guidebook: Read Philippians 1:6.

FISHING: After a cold front moves through, downsize your lures and fish them more slowly.

2. WHAT IS CONTENTMENT?

"Godliness with contentment is great gain."
1 TIMOTHY 6:6

I've seen many changes during my 30-plus years as an outdoor journalist. The advances in hunting equipment have been nothing short of amazing. Thirty years ago, camouflage clothing, single cam bows, and stainless rifles were unheard of. Today they are the rage of the hunting industry, replacing the time-tested hunting products that had served hunters well for decades.

With the emergence of new hunting products, sportsmen started being fed the idea that one's hunting prowess and contentment could only be measured by the size of the animals harvested. As this mindset gained a foothold, the whole concept of hunter contentment began to change. In the eyes of a growing number of sportsmen, contentment in the field was no longer measured by a day in the woods. Results were what mattered most. Unfortunately, this has led to a host of problems, with greed and lust being the biggest.

FAST FACT:
Charlie's photos have graced the covers of dozens of magazines, including Field & Stream, Sports Afield, Outdoor Life, *and* Deer and Deer Hunting.

Rather than focusing on antlers and success, hunters should realize that contentment is not about the prize, it's about experiencing the blessings we can derive from God's creation—the sunrises and sunsets, the smells of fallen leaves in an autumn forest, the bite felt from a cold frosty morning in a deer stand, and the rustling sound of a deer walking on a bed of dried leaves. And if one is fortunate enough to harvest a deer in the process, that's just frosting on the cake.

—Charles Alsheimer

FOLLOW THE COMPASS

In your occupation, what is your definition of success? Have you ever thought of it in terms of how you honor God and how you can stay content in the middle of the tough times?

From the Guidebook: Read Matthew 6:19–24

HUNTING: Never trust the safety on your gun. It is a mechanical device that can fail.

3. HUNTER SAFETY

"All Scripture is God-breathed and is useful for teaching, rebuking, correcting and training in righteousness."

2 TIMOTHY 3:16

For the last several years our Sportsperson's Club has been teaching hunter safety.

During the 12 hours of instruction, a variety of topics are covered but all deal with safety. Some are focused on safe gun handling; others are directed more toward safety in bow hunting. Others deal with survival skills, and we also include a simulated field course. Although this is a required course, most students seem eager to learn.

FAST FACT:

In Michigan, where Maury teaches the safety class, among the things students learn are shooting skills, hunting skills, primitive hunting (muzzleloaders and bows), and survival skills.

In hunter safety there is a manual that we cover carefully during the course.

There is another manual that many of us tend to neglect. It was also designed for our safety—safe living now and safety in the future. This manual is the Bible.

The Bible can do many things for us. It can teach us the best way to live. It can help us to understand when we go off the track. It can give us instructions for how to get back on the right road. It can provide us with the equipment for living in the right way.

But the Bible isn't just another good book. It is a special book given to us by God himself. It is His Word. He breathed it out by His Spirit and people wrote it down. "All Scripture is God-breathed," 2 Timothy 3:16 tells us, "and is useful for teaching, rebuking, correcting and training in righteousness, so that the man of God may be thoroughly equipped for every good work."

Each student is willing and eager to learn safe practices for hunting. Are we that way with God's instructions? Are we concerned about how we can live safely now and how we can be safe in the future? The Bible is our true safety manual.

—MAURY DE YOUNG

FOLLOW THE COMPASS

What biblical principles or teachings do you know of that can help you live your life more safely?

From the Guidebook: Read Psalm 119:89–96.

HUNTER SAFETY: Treat every gun as a loaded gun.

4. LIFE-SAVING CHOICE

*"What good will it be for a man if he gains
the whole world, yet forfeits his soul?"*

MATTHEW 16:26

W ho would ever dream of amputating his own leg? Nobody—unless that person had lost his mind or was faced with the grim choice of losing either his leg or his life.

That was Bill Jeracki's terrible predicament, according to the *Denver Post*, when he was out fishing all alone in the foothills of the Rocky Mountains. He was trapped when a boulder fell on his leg, and he was unable to free himself.

FAST FACT:
*According to
some sources,
eye injuries while
fishing have sur-
passed all other
sports in the
number of such
injuries.*

Knowing that as night came on he might die of exposure, Bill did what he knew he had to do. Relying on his skill as an assistant to a doctor at a Denver hospital, he took a nylon rope out of his tackle box, tied it tightly above his knee, and cut off his leg with his knife. He then dragged himself to his car and drove 10 miles to the nearest town. He not only survived the trauma, but with an artificial limb he is out fishing again.

What a decision—your leg or your life!

But what if the stakes were even higher? Suppose you had to choose between giving up some habit, ambition, or relationship, and giving up heaven. The Lord made the issue of following Him that decisive. He said, "What good will it be for a man if he gains the whole world, yet forfeits his soul?" (Matthew 16:26). It's a question you and I must answer.

—VERNON GROUNDS

FOLLOW THE COMPASS

Are you sure that your soul has been redeemed—that you are destined for heaven? It's the most important decision you will ever make. Trust Jesus as Savior today.

From the Guidebook: Read Matthew 16:13–28

HUNTING: Wear layers of clothing when hunting so you can adjust to rising and falling temperatures.

5. WEAKNESSES AND STRENGTHS

On Point:
Turning problems into opportunities

"[Their] weakness was turned to strength;
and [they] became powerful in battle."

HEBREWS 11:34

I'm always amused when I watch the loons lift into flight off Piatt Lake in Michigan's Upper Peninsula. They half-run, half-flap across the water for hundreds of feet before getting enough speed to lift into the air. I wondered why it takes so much effort—until I learned that unlike most birds, loons have solid bones. Their added weight makes it difficult for them to get airborne.

FAST FACT:

Sometimes when they are migrating, loons mistake parking lots for lakes and land on them. They then have a difficult time getting airborne again because they need a long water runway with which to take off.

I also learned that loons are clumsy on land because their legs are set farther back on their bodies than other birds. Walking is so difficult that many loons simply scoot across land to their nesting places. But these disadvantages—heavy bones, legs set far back—are also tremendous advantages. Because of their weight and leg placement, loons can dive deeper, farther, and faster. This is essential for catching fish and escaping predators.

What we see as disadvantages in our lives can be turned into advantages, and apparent weaknesses can be transformed into strengths. That was true of the apostle Paul, whose "thorn in the flesh" became an opportunity for God's strength to be seen in his weakness (2 Corinthians 12:7–9). And it was true of the Old Testament heroes mentioned in Hebrews 11.

What "weakness" is holding you down? Is it shyness or a physical limitation? Ask God to turn it into a strength for His glory.

— DAVID EGNER

FOLLOW THE COMPASS

What disadvantages in life do you have—weaknesses that God can turn into strengths? Do you trust Him to be able to do that?

From the Guidebook: 2 Corinthians 12:1–10

HUNTING/FISHING: Sharpening a knife blade only takes a few minutes if done regularly and can make hunting, fishing, and camping tasks simple. A dull knife, however, could take close to an hour to sharpen and doesn't perform skinning or cutting tasks well. Sharpen your knives regularly.

6. ROUGH GOING

*"In this world you will have trouble. But take heart!
I have overcome the world."*

JOHN 16:33

There's a lake near our home in the mountains that is known for good fishing. To get there, I had to hike two miles up a steep ridge—a hard climb for an old-timer like me. But then I discovered that it's possible to drive within a half-mile of the lake. I spent most of a day driving several mountain roads until I found the one that got me the closest. Then I carefully mapped the road so I could find it again.

FAST FACT:
David Roper lives in Boise, Idaho, in the foothills of the Rocky Mountains.

Several months later, I drove the road again. I came to a section that was much worse than I remembered—rocky, rutted, and steep. I wondered if I had missed a turn, so I stopped and checked my map. There, penciled alongside the stretch on which I was driving, were the words: "Rough and steep. Hard going." I was on the right road.

Jesus said that our life's journey will be rough going if we choose to follow Him. "In this world you will have trouble" (John 16:33). So we shouldn't be surprised if our path becomes difficult, nor should we believe we've taken a wrong turn. We can "take heart" because Jesus also said that in Him we can have peace, for He has "overcome the world" (v. 33).

If you're following Christ and experiencing some bumpy times, take heart—you're on the right road!

—DAVID ROPER

FOLLOW THE COMPASS

What is the "rough and steep" part of your life right now? What are you learning about God as you experience this?

From the Guidebook: Read John 16:19–33.

HUNTING: If you want to get kids involved in hunting, don't have them start hunting deer or animals that require sitting for long periods of time. Introduce them to squirrel or rabbit hunting first. Fast-paced hunting that includes walking around in the woods will keep them interested in outdoor sports.

7. CHECK THE COMPASS

*"See if there is any offensive way in me,
and lead me in the way everlasting."*

PSALM 139:24

Two Florida men charted a course and drove their fishing boat out into the Gulf of Mexico. Using the boat's compass, they headed to deep waters 60 miles offshore where they hoped to catch some grouper. When they arrived at what they thought was the right place, they turned on their depth finder and realized they were nowhere near their target. They discovered that one of them had laid a flashlight near the ship's compass, and the attached magnet had affected the reading.

FAST FACT:

Most experts agree that using a compass without an accompanying map is not going to do you any good while you try to get oriented.

Just as that magnet changed the compass, so our sinful hearts can influence our thinking. Many of Jesus' countrymen, for example, thought they were moving in the right direction by denying that He was the promised Messiah (John 7:41–42). But the real problem with these people was the bias in their hearts. They resisted Jesus because of the threat He seemed to pose to their religious traditions. Rather than carefully checking all the Scriptures, which would have verified who He was, they settled for what they preferred to believe. As a result, they rejected the One who had come to save them.

Because we too can be self-deceived, we must ask the Lord to expose the inner motives that cast shadows across our minds, dim our spiritual discernment (Psalm 139:24), and affect our spiritual compass. With God's help, we can get back on course in our pursuit of godly living.

—MART DE HAAN

FOLLOW THE COMPASS

Have you heard the dissenting comments of those who reject Jesus? How have you learned to counter those attacks? How important is it to you to do this?

From the Guidebook: Read John 7:37–53.

FISHING: When using a two-piece fishing rod, take extra care that the sections remain securely in place. They tend to come loose when you cast many times. Use a small amount of paraffin wax on the metal ring at the tip of the rod before joining the two pieces.

8. HERE TODAY, GONE TOMORROW

"Even though I walk through the valley of the shadow of death, I will fear no evil, for you are with me; your rod and your staff, they comfort me."

PSALM 23:4

One of my most memorable (and worst) hunting trips was when I went turkey hunting and had a shotgun accident. The hunt started like any other day in the field chasing gobblers, but it ended with me alone and crawling out of the woods. I had to crawl out of the woods using very little of my left leg because of a large shotgun blast just above my knee. My right leg is affected by cerebral palsy, so I couldn't walk.

FAST FACT:
To read more about the author and a variety of Christian outdoor-related articles, visit www.tracy breen.com.

As I dragged my body about a third of a mile to my car and wondered if I would be alive in ten minutes, hunting and other things didn't seem as important as they usually do. What became clear to me was the importance of my relationship with God and my family. I stopped wondering about how long the beard on the gobbler that I was watching a few minutes ago was. I wondered how my wife and young son would survive without a husband and a father.

Near-death experiences put things into perspective and make us realize how important relationships are and how unimportant other things are. We spend much of our lives chasing after the things that don't matter. Is there a relationship that you have neglected because work, sports, or other things have been placed on a pedestal instead of focusing on the things that matter? Take the time to put them first.

—TRACY BREEN

FOLLOW THE COMPASS

Is there a relationship that you have neglected because something else got in the way? What can you do to mend that relationship? How can you make sure that relationships continue to be the priority in your life?

From the Guidebook: Read Psalm 23.

HUNTING: Use reflective ties if tracking at night. This will help you see a pattern and also keep you from heading back on the same trail you are following. Make sure you remove the ties later.

9. A FISHERMAN'S PRAYER

*" 'Come, follow me,' Jesus said, 'and I will
make you fishers of men.' "*

MATTHEW 4:19

I'm sure we've all heard them before. You probably have a good one. Fish stories—tall tales about the one that got away. An anonymous writer scribbled down a poem called "The Fishermen's Prayer." It goes like this:

"Dear God, please let me catch a fish so big that even I, when boasting of it afterwards, will have no need to tell a lie."

FAST FACT:

Although the actual World's Largest Muskie title is bogged down in contro-versy, the biggest ever weighed in at somewhere around 70 pounds.

My story of the big one that got away comes from back when I was a kid. My dad, brother, and I were up early one summer morning on Hiawatha Lake in Michigan. A monster pulled my bobber under for what seemed like minutes. I started crankin' away on my little Zebco 202 reel, and the giant fish surfaced. It had to have been three feet long! (Seriously, I'm not lying!) My dad said, "It's a Muskie"! But before he could surface again, my pole snapped back, and Mr. Muskie was gone. We never saw it again.

This story of fishing got me thinking about what Jesus said in Matthew 4 about being fish-ers of men. He was talking about our witness, our lifestyle. For a long time, I've got to admit it, that verse scared me. I thought we had to convince people to follow Christ by using our intellect and reasoning. However, God has been showing me through His Word what's involved in fishing for men (Romans 10:14–16, John 16:7–9).

All we do is cast on the surface of society's water. The Holy Spirit moves a person spiritually to make the strike. Our lives become a "lure" when we live for Christ in obedience and faith.

Maybe our fisherman's prayer should be, "Lord, make me a fisher of men."

— Dan Deal

FOLLOW THE COMPASS

At school, work, or at home with family, don't worry about the response people have to your testimony. Just present yourself to God as a "living lure," a sacrifice that the Holy Spirit can use to catch the souls of men by your witness.

From the Guidebook: Paul's message in 2 Corinthians 4 will revitalize your testimony for Christ with the power of the cross. If you can, go deeper still in John 16.

FISHING WITH KIDS: Catching several small panfish will hold kids' attention and develop their interest in fishing much more than going after the bigger ones.

10. NOW FOR THE HARD PART

*"When Jesus saw their faith, he said,
'Friend, your sins are forgiven.'"*

LUKE 5:20

One of the worst parts of fishing is cleaning your catch. It's a dirty job, but someone has to do it.

In my family, that someone is usually me. I'll never forget the time my wife and I went fishing in Tampa Bay. It was one of those fishing trips where everything clicked. Fish after fish struck our bait. By the end of the day, our arms ached from fighting and landing dozens of fish, but I didn't care. I was having too much fun—until it came time to clean the fish. Then the fun ended and the work began.

FAST FACT:
Today there are about 35 species of fish living in the Sea of Galilee.

Jesus knew a lot about fishing. He lived on the Sea of Galilee, where many of his friends made their living catching fish. In fact, He invited His fishermen friends to trade in their nets and become fishers of men. And by extension, He invites us to take up the same task—fishing for men. He wants us to seek out those we might lead to Him for rescue.

One of the best things about being a fisher of men is that we don't have to clean what we catch. God does the cleaning (Luke 5:21; 1 John 1:9). Of course, we are called at times to invite people to change by playing the role of encourager or confronter, but it's not our job to "clean" or restore anyone. That's God's business.

To a fisherman (both marine and human) such as I am, it's a relief to know that I don't bear the responsibility to change those I have the privilege of seeing firsthand place their faith in Christ. My job is simply to cast the net.

—JEFF OLSON

FOLLOW THE COMPASS

Set a goal to become a better fisher of men. How can you find better ways to lead friends to Jesus—and let Him do the cleanup?

From the Guidebook: Read Luke 5:1–11.

FISHING WITH KIDS: Buy the best equipment you can find that fits them. They can get discouraged easily by equipment that does not work well.

11. CAMPFIRES AND CHURCHES

*"Let us consider how we may spur
one another on toward love."*

HEBREWS 10:24

Campfires are an everyday experience in the outdoor world. This dates back to years ago when meals were cooked over a fire but moves ahead to the present time when just the sound of the word *campfire* may bring to mind the pleasant aroma of burning wood or the delicious taste of a marshmallow or a "s'more."

Various methods are used to put a fire out. Some fires are in safe containers and people just let them burn until they are out of fuel. Sometimes there is water nearby, and one can douse it with water. But in high country, one of the common methods is to separate the coals. Coals glow brightly and give us much heat when several of them are close together, but when they are separated they lose their heat and eventually the fire goes out.

Separate the coals, and the fire goes out!

In my own life I have grown to appreciate and see the need for other warm, glowing coals being close to me! For a time, "Jesus and me" may have something going, but over the long haul, I need other Christians. I need people who will pray for me, encourage me, challenge me, and hold me accountable. That's where

FAST FACT:
Want to build a better campfire? Most sources say to build a cabin of sticks around the outside and place a teepee of sticks inside that.

a good church comes into play, and if I can be more specific, a good Bible-believing church that stresses small groups.

Hebrews 10:24–25 says, "Let us consider how we may spur one another on toward love and good deeds. Let us not give up meeting together, as some are in the habit of doing, but let us encourage one another."

Do you sense the need for good, wholesome relationships? The right kind of church is a good place for this to happen. Gather the coals together, and keep your fire burning.

—Maury De Young

FOLLOW THE COMPASS

Do you have three or four people you consider close Christian friends? Do you have a church where you feel your fire for the Lord is fanned and made to glow brighter? If not, what should you do?

From the Guidebook: Read Acts 2:42–47.

HUNTING: In selecting a place for a tree stand, look for funnels or edges between a food source and bedding area. Funnels are places where the habitat narrows down to a crossing area for deer. Deer usually move along the side of a hill near the top.

12. THEY AREN'T HUNGRY!

"Blessed are those who hunger and thirst for righteousness."
MATTHEW 5:6

Everything was all set for the first bass fishing expedition of the year. We had some exotic new lures that we just knew would be irresistible to those big 6-pounders lurking beneath the surface of our favorite fishing lake. We would tempt them with Sassy Shads, with new brightly colored Hula Poppers, with buzz baits, with a "killer" red flatfish with a black stripe, and with a white double spinner with long bright streamers. And, if all else failed, we had some fresh Canadian crawlers. We were out at dawn, hitting all the best spots with our assortment of delectable temptations. But nothing happened. We worked the shore. We cast along the weeds. We tried every lure in the tackle box—even the crawlers. Finally we gave up. As we motored back to the cabin, we concluded, "The fish just aren't hungry."

Come to think of it, I see some parallels in our ongoing battle against temptation. Satan has a whole "tacklebox" of alluring devices he uses to tempt us. Some of them are gaudy and exotic, easy to spot—yet oh, so tempting! Others are designed to whet our appetites in quiet and subtle ways, appearing innocent until the hook is set. Whatever the temptation, we can best resist if we do not let our thoughts

FAST FACT:
A Sassy Shad makes trophy game fish go crazy, because it looks like a little fish swimming along in the water—exactly what a big old bass is looking for—if he's hungry.

dwell on evil but on things that are true, noble, just, pure, and lovely (Philippians 4:8). With mental discipline and the help of the Holy Spirit, we can keep our hearts full of goodness. Then, in frustration, Satan will have to say, "They just aren't hungry!"

—David Egner

FOLLOW THE COMPASS

What lure of Satan seems attractive to you? Do you think you can miss the hooks and get by with going for his tricks? Ask God to help you avoid the temptations of the enemy.

From the Guidebook: Read James 1:12–18.

HUNTING: Put some scent on top of your boot some distance from your stand. You might be surprised when you see a buck following your footsteps.

13. TROUBLE IS COMING

*"Man is born to trouble as surely
as sparks fly upward."*

JOB 5:7

Trouble is inevitable. It's not a matter of *if* it will come, but *when*. My friend Tracy's hunting trip reminded me of this.

Tracy Breen is a freelance outdoor writer and photographer. You'll recognize him as one of the other writers in this book. Part of Tracy's job is to spend time in the field, testing the latest hunting gear and writing stories about his experiences. It's a tough job, but hey, he's willing to do it.

FAST FACT:

Ben Franklin preferred the turkey to the bald eagle as the national bird of the US.

When he was out in the woods of Northern Michigan hunting turkeys a few years ago, however, trouble found him. One minute, he's hunting gobblers and enjoying God's great outdoors. The next, he's shot in the upper leg and struggling for life.

Tracy is still not entirely sure how it all happened, but his 12-gauge shotgun accidentally went off and the pellets struck him just above the knee of his "good" leg. You see, Tracy suffers from a lifelong battle with cerebral palsy. The childhood disease left him crippled in his right leg. He can still walk, but he labors with every step.

With both legs now debilitated, Tracy crawled through the woods nearly a third of a mile to get help. Fortunately, God was watching out for him, and the gunshot wound was not fatal.

Tracy's ordeal has been a humbling, eye-opening experience. Even someone like him, who is no stranger to suffering, can tend to think he is invincible. But none of us is (Job 5:7).

Jesus told His followers, "In this world you will have trouble." But he also urged them to *take heart* when trouble finds them because He has "overcome the world" (John 16:33).

—JEFF OLSON

FOLLOW THE COMPASS

Where do you think that you are invincible to trouble? Realistically, how invincible do you really think you are?

For Further Study: Check out Tracy Breen's Web site www.tracybreen.com.

HUNTING: When hiking off the beaten path, take a lightweight tarp with you. Tarps have several purposes. They can serve as an emergency shelter if a storm blows through an area or serve as an overnight shelter if you get lost. Putting a tarp on the ground when boning out meat keeps the dirt and debris off the meat.

14. A FISHING FINALITY!

"Now I am about to go the way of all the earth. You know with all your heart and soul that not one of all the good promises the Lord your God gave you has failed."

JOSHUA 23:14

Fishing is a calculating and often temperamental sport.

One must figure out exactly what the fish are striking at to be successful. One day you find plastic worms are working; the next, it's a deep-diving jig. Other days, good ol' crickets are what the fish are feeding on. You never know what the day will hold, and you must adapt each and every time to weather patterns, feeding patterns, water temperature, and a number of other factors.

FAST FACT:
An example of what bait works best: For perch, according to fishing guy Robin Radford, try minnows, worms, crayfish, insect larvae, insects, small flies, ice spoons, and small jigs.

The human race is just as fickle. Every day holds a different story, and every day we experience changing emotions and outcomes. The good news is that God is stable and constant day in and day out. We don't have to figure God out every day. His Word portrays consistency and is something we can feed on each day, no matter what has changed since the last.

We see this in the proclamation about God's promises in Joshua 23:14. They were good to go back then, and they are good to go today.

Remember God's consistency the next time you hit the streams, and be grateful that God's promises and love are not like those fish you are trying to catch.

—ERIC JONES

FOLLOW THE COMPASS

Think of some situations in which you have sensed God's constant care in your life. Spend a few minutes today thanking Him for taking care of you in that way.

From the Guidebook: Read Joshua 23.

FISHING: Use glue to attach the plastic tail to the jig head. This helps it to stay on longer than just attaching the plastic tail to the hook.

15. LOSS OF DIRECTION

*"Great peace have they who love your law,
and nothing can make them stumble."*

PSALM 119:165

Two men had been out deep-sea fishing when night began to fall. As they headed back toward land, the more experienced seaman got sleepy and turned the helm over to his friend. The veteran sailor pointed out the North Star and said, "Just keep the boat going in that direction."

FAST FACT:

Polaris, the North Star, is not the brightest star in the sky; Sirius is the brightest.

The man had not been at his task very long before he too fell asleep. When he awoke, he was thoroughly confused. He shook his friend frantically and shouted, "Wake up and show me another star! I've run clean past that first one!"

Many people today are looking for something new to guide their lives because they've lost sight of God's standard. They regard the Bible as a relic from the past and no longer dependable. But God's laws are just as relevant and practical now as when He first gave them.

His standards are more constant than the North Star and as unfailing as the law of gravity. They are not arbitrary rules like the traffic laws that tell us whether to drive on the right side of the road or the left.

To violate God's commands brings destruction to individuals and chaos to society. But to observe His words brings this comforting result: "Great peace have they who love your law" (Psalm 119:165).

—HADDON ROBINSON

FOLLOW THE COMPASS

How do you view the Bible? Do you see it as your guide for truth and for how to live? Spend some time examining the veracity and reliability of this book.

From the Guidebook: Read Psalm 119:161–168.

HUNTING/FISHING: Always keep a compass handy in case your GPS stops working or the batteries go dead.

16. THE EYES OF COMPASSION

"Someone urged me to kill you. But my eye spared you."
1 SAMUEL 24:10 (NKJV)

When a Michigan deer hunter found a 100-pound buck struggling to get out of a mud-bog in which it was hopelessly stuck, the hunter couldn't bring himself to squeeze the trigger. Instead, he and his hunting partner snared the animal with a rope and pulled it out of the mud. The deer then bolted to freedom.

The hunter later recalled, "When you see a deer like that, eyeball to eyeball, it's a little different. I think the eyes did it, that longing look, as if to say, 'What are you going to do?' "

FAST FACT:
Michigan has an estimated deer population of more than 1.5 million.

This account bears an interesting parallel to the incident recorded in 1 Samuel 24. Saul was in a defenseless situation when David and his armed men found him in a cave. David had good reason to kill Saul. Yet he showed mercy. He knew that the Lord had made Saul king of Israel, and he was not about to take the life of the Lord's anointed—even though it would have been easy (v. 10).

Suppose someone who has hurt you in the past suddenly became vulnerable. Would your reaction be to hurt him? Or would you be compassionate and reverent like David, who recognized that judgment and vengeance belong to the Lord? (v. 12). Let's look at others through the eyes of mercy.

—MART DE HAAN

FOLLOW THE COMPASS

Is there someone in your life who has hurt you recently? Are you willing to help that person if he or she is in trouble, or do you view this person as someone who is getting what is deserved?

From the Guidebook: Read 1 Samuel 24:1–15.

HUNTING: Studies show that many deer hunters are at risk of having a heart attack while in the field. Dragging out a deer, long strenuous walks, and buck fever can cause a heart attack. To reduce the chances of having heart trouble, don't eat a large breakfast before hunting. This can actually reduce the blood flow to the heart.

17. WHO MADE IT?

"He made the earth by his power; he founded the world by his wisdom and stretched out the heavens by his understanding."

JEREMIAH 51:15

I'd spent the morning climbing high into Alberta's sheep country. Upon reaching the crest of a ridge, I was treated to a breathtaking scene. Stretched out before me were snow-capped mountains as far as the eye could see. There was no sound but the wind. In this part of the world man didn't play a role—it belonged to God and His creatures.

FAST FACT:

You can take a look at some of the sheep Charles photographed. Go to his Web site: www. charliealsheimer. com.

Below in a bowl on the side of the mountain were several bighorn rams—some bedded, some feeding. Fearing the sheep would spook, I quickly mounted my camera on the tripod and began taking photos. As the minutes passed, the sheep calmed to my presence, allowing me to move among them as if I were invisible. The experience was something all sheep hunters and wildlife photographers dream of having.

As the day wound down I stretched out in an alpine meadow to reflect before heading off the mountain. A myriad of thoughts raced through my mind while taking in all that lay before me. Every thought drew me to the same conclusion. The day's events were a gift from God.

The fact that some people doubt that God made planet earth is hard to fathom. Creation is meant to lead us to God. And part of our journey is in understanding that God sent His son Jesus to earth, to show us the way.

—CHARLES ALSHEIMER

FOLLOW THE COMPASS

Take some time to study Jeremiah 51:15. What great truths can you gain from that verse—truths to help you through the day?

From the Guidebook: Read Psalm 95:4–5.

HUNTING: Use as few hunting gadgets as possible. The fewer gadgets you use the less chance there is of something malfunctioning.

18. QUALITY CONTROL

"Each of us should please his neighbor for his good, to build him up."

ROMANS 15:2

Many deer hunters have worked hard to build up the quality of deer hunting in their area. They have worked to gain a better buck-to-doe ratio. They have let small bucks go to see them grow. Their goal is to build up the quality of the deer herd in that area, so they can later harvest more mature bucks.

FAST FACT:

Quality Deer Management involves the protection of younger bucks, combined with an adequate harvest of female deer to maintain a healthy population in balance with habitat conditions and landowner desires.

I personally endorse much of this view, but I do not want to limit young hunters in harvesting their first deer or their first buck.

The Bible talks about building up something that will result in better quality as well. It tells us that we need to "please our neighbor for his good, to build him up." If we say things and do things that build up our spouse, our kids, our fellow workers, and our friends, we will be amazed at the improved quality of our relationships.

It is so easy to do things that please ourselves instead of focusing on what will please our neighbor. It is so easy to cut our neighbor down instead of building him or her up. Our normal tendency is to build ourselves up as we put down those around us. We have also experienced the damage that these tendencies can bring.

Let's practice what the Bible says. By building each other up with words and actions, we will be able to enjoy the higher quality of relationships that result.

—Maury De Young

FOLLOW THE COMPASS

Reflect on your relationships. How much of your focus is on pleasing yourself and building yourself up? How much of your conversation and actions really pleases those around you and builds them up?

From the Guidebook: Read Hebrews 3:13 and 10:24.

HUNTING: Do not use a grunt call on the ground when it is dark. You might find yourself between two charging bucks.

19. ICE FISHING

"You shall have no other gods before me."

EXODUS 20:3

Two Texans went to Minnesota one winter to do some ice fishing. After setting up their tent, they pulled the cord on their chain saw to cut a hole in the ice. Then they heard a mysterious voice from above saying, "There are no fish under the ice."

"Is that You, God?" they asked in awe.

"No," came the reply, "but I know that there are no fish under the ice. I'm the owner of this ice-skating rink."

People who worship gods other than the one true God resemble fishermen ice fishing in a skating rink. The idolaters of Isaiah's day worked hard at practicing their religion. They spent exorbitant sums of money overlaying their professionally carved idols with gold and crafting silver chains for them (Isaiah 40:19–20). They bowed down and worshiped what they had constructed with their own hands (Psalm 115:4–7). Yet, there was nothing there. They appeared to be worshiping God, but their worship was as futile as fishing in an ice-skating rink.

Our great God can never be reduced to an image of man's own making. "The Lord is the everlasting God, the Creator of the ends of the earth" (Isaiah 40:28). And He wants us to worship Him in spirit and in truth (John 4:24).

—HADDON ROBINSON

FAST FACT:

According to the US Army Cold Regions research labs, it takes four inches of solid ice to support a one-ton load on a frozen body of water.

FOLLOW THE COMPASS

What do you find as the best way of worshiping God? Do you sometimes find that you can worship him while out hunting or even ice fishing?

From the Guidebook: Read Psalm 115:1–11.

ICE FISHING: A power auger will allow you to drill a bigger hole faster, but it will also drive off the fish you want to hook.

20. DON'T WAIT TOO LONG!

"Isaac said, 'I am now an old man and don't know the day of my death.'"
GENESIS 27:2

Most of us wait as long as we can before confronting the painful aspects of life. When we have something really difficult or distasteful to do, we usually put it off until the last possible second. This is not only true of dental appointments and mortgage payments but also of our preparation for death. A great many people wait as long as they can before they accept the fact that they are going to die. But there's danger in delay! They need to prepare today to meet God.

FAST FACT:

The lost-hunter illustration should remind all hunters to carry a cell phone into the woods. Disoriented hunters have been tracked by their phones—and lives have been saved. Just turn it off before actually hunting.

While deer hunting in Michigan's Upper Peninsula, I experienced the sinking feeling that comes from waiting too long before taking action. I usually walked quite far into the woods, but while daylight remained I could always find my way back to the road. On my last night of hunting, though, I lingered in the forest an extra 20 minutes, hoping for that big buck. It seemed I was suddenly surrounded by darkness. Nothing looked familiar. Clouds obscured the moon. Momentarily I panicked. Because I had paused too long, I was lost.

Similarly, some people do not see the onsetting darkness of death until it's too late. They believe there is time to decide, that some daylight is left. Perhaps there is, but how soon night falls! I found my way out of that Michigan darkness, but there's no escape from the blackness of eternal night.

Have you been putting off your decision to receive Christ as Savior and Lord of your life? Don't wait too long! Believe in Him now.

—DAVID EGNER

FOLLOW THE COMPASS

Perhaps you already know Jesus as Savior. But is there some other spiritual decision you've been putting off? Why not do the right thing today?

From the Guidebook: Read Job 21:23–32.

HUNTING SAFETY: For pre-dawn or post-dusk hunting, take along a small flashlight—it lets other hunters know that you are a human. And it might come in handy if you need to hike out after dark.

21. LOONS OR EAGLES?

*"Do not get drunk on wine, which leads to debauchery.
Instead, be filled with the Spirit."*

EPHESIANS 5:18

When I was a lad, my father was my "authority" on the world of nature. One day as we were talking about those birds from which we get the expression "crazy as a loon," he mentioned that without any wind blowing it was almost impossible for them to take off and fly. I took his word for it, but it didn't seem to make sense to me until one evening some time later when my brother and I were out fishing. Not a breeze was stirring and the surface of the small lake was like glass. The quietness of the moment was suddenly broken by the loud flapping of wings. Evidently we had scared "Mr. Loon," and he decided to get out of there. Yet, despite his heroic effort, he just skimmed along the surface of the water—unable to gain altitude.

FAST FACT:

It's easy to go online and find loon calls on YouTube or other Internet sites.

Reaching the other side of the lake, he still wasn't high enough to clear the trees. He made a fancy turn and came back toward us, still flapping his wings with all his might. We held our breath as he reached the opposite shore, barely missed the treetops, and disappeared from view. He made it—but what a struggle!

Recalling that experience, the thought came to me: What a contrast there is between that struggling loon and the majestic eagle that ascends high in the heavens with wings outstretched, gliding effortlessly to new and thrilling heights. The flapping loon and the soaring eagle portray two kinds of Christians. There are some dear souls who seem to be always "flapping" without making much headway, while others can truthfully and joyfully sing with the hymn writer, "New heights I'm gaining every day." The latter are those who have learned to wait upon the Lord, have renewed their strength, and hence "soar on wings like eagles" (Isaiah 40:31).

Do you have a Spirit-filled life? Do you rest upon the Lord and let Him work through you? When others see you, are they reminded of flapping loons or soaring eagles?

—RICHARD DE HAAN

FOLLOW THE COMPASS

What would it mean to "soar" in your Christian experience? What are some steps you need to take to become a soaring believer?

From the Guidebook: Read Galatians 5:16–26.

HUNTING: If you have trouble seeing where your arrows are hitting in low light conditions, purchase lighted nocks. There are many brands available that are extremely bright. As your buck disappears into the brush, you will know exactly where the arrow hit.

22. WORK OPPORTUNITY

"As servants of God we commend ourselves in every way: in great endurance; in troubles, hardships and distresses."

2 CORINTHIANS 6:4

Imagine yourself as an 18-year-old hunting through the want ads for summer work. Because you like the outdoors, your interest is drawn to an ad run by the Upper Mississippi River National Wildlife and Fish Refuge. It advertises job openings in its youth conservation program. But that isn't all it offers. The ad also promises that the work will include "exposure to heat, humidity, rain, mud, millions of biting mosquitoes, poison plants, barbed wire, and hard work." The pay is minimum wage. The program director who actually ran such an ad was quoted as saying, "This isn't going to be one of those programs where you play darts at government expense."

Now imagine that the 18-year-old is a Christian looking for meaningful spiritual service for the Lord. His eyes rest thoughtfully upon the sixth chapter of 2 Corinthians. There he finds the apostle Paul describing the highest calling of all, an opportunity to work together with the Lord. But here again the job description is very candid about some of the stresses that go with the work. While Paul's experiences as an apostle were unique, his words remind all readers that

FAST FACT:

The Upper Mississippi Refuge is comprised of 233,000 acres of wooded islands, marshes, and back-waters. It is located in the Mississippi River Valley from Wabasha, Minnesota, to Rock Island, Illinois.

serving the Lord in any capacity is not one big vacation. It requires great care and effort. It takes the highest commitment and utmost personal sacrifice.

Yes, the challenge of serving Christ is without parallel and may tax us to our limits. But we are not in it alone, and this makes all the difference. No price is too great to pay for the privilege of working with and for the Lord!

—MART DE HAAN

FOLLOW THE COMPASS

What service for the Lord do you feel He is calling you to provide? What is the cost to you? What are the rewards? Are you ready?

From the Guidebook: Read 2 Corinthians 6:1–10.

HUNTING SAFETY: If possible, copy off a satellite shot of your hunting grounds to help you know where you are and to help avoid getting lost.

23. SURPRISE!

*"For you know very well that the day of the Lord
will come like a thief in the night."*

I THESSALONIANS 5:2

FAST FACT:

*Muscles next to
the scent glands
of skunks enable
them to spray with
a high degree of
accuracy from 7
to 15 feet. Their
offensive odor can
be detected down-
wind by humans
as far as a mile
away.*

Entering the woods early one morning, eager to get to my tree stand, I turned on my flashlight. I kept the light down so as not to disturb any deer, but I needed the light to avoid dead branches, or I would spook the deer going in. I had the light about three feet from the ground pointing down. Suddenly in my light I noticed something that didn't seem quite right. There was a real dark, almost black object there. I looked again and noticed that there was a white stripe down the back of this black animal!

I believe I set a record turning off the light and moving away from that skunk. I didn't want to run, as I thought that might spook him more. I slithered away as quickly as possible. As I moved away I heard the pitter patter of feet going the opposite direction. I don't know who was more surprised, the skunk or me, but thankfully, he left no odor as he moved away.

The Bible tells us that Jesus is coming back again, and this day will come as a surprise. It will be just like a thief coming in the night, when we don't expect it.

We don't know if we will meet Jesus when we die or if He will return before we die, but either way the important plan is to be prepared before it happens. Are you prepared to meet Him?

—MAURY DE YOUNG

FOLLOW THE COMPASS

If you were to meet Jesus tonight, would you be prepared? Are there any changes that should take place first, while you still have the opportunity?

From the Guidebook: Read 2 Peter 3 and Revelation 3:3.

HUNTING: The sense of smell for most big game animals is hundreds of times better than the human nose. Animals often smell us and anything we touch as we walk through the woods. To reduce human odor left in the woods, always wear rubber boots, scent-free gloves and store your hunting clothes in a scent-free container when you're not hunting.

24. LOCAL FISH MANAGEMENT

"For we are not unaware of [Satan's] schemes."
2 CORINTHIANS 2:11

Recently, I watched a couple of boys fishing on a small lake in the Upper Peninsula of Michigan. As I peered out the cabin window, I noticed one of them reeling in a decent sized fish. I found myself smiling as the boy muscled it to the edge of their small boat.

For a second, I looked down to take a sip of coffee. When I looked up, I could see the boy hammering away at something alongside of the boat. Puzzled, I turned to my friend and asked what the boy was doing. Grinning, he explained the boy was practicing "local fish management." Apparently, northern pike had invaded the lake and were threatening to overtake the fish population. So the locals were practicing their own method of fish management.

FAST FACT:
Wildlife officials have tried various poisons and explosives to rid lakes of overpopulated pike.

While their methods were a bit on the barbaric side, I found myself respecting how seriously they took the threat. They didn't pretend it didn't exist. They didn't naively hope it would go away. They saw the threat for what it was and took action!

Watching them challenged me to consider how seriously I take threats in my life, in particular, the greatest threat of all—Satan (Ephesians 6:12). The Bible warns us, "Your enemy the devil prowls around like a roaring lion looking for someone to devour. Resist him, standing firm in the faith" (1 Peter 5:8–9).

Stay alert! Satan, the "father of lies," will try to invade the water of our lives with lies intended to overtake us.

How seriously are you taking him as a threat?

—JEFF OLSON

FOLLOW THE COMPASS

What are some of the common lies Satan is trying to sell you that you need to resist? Are there any lies you have agreed with that you need to break?

For Further Reading: Read the Discovery Series booklet *When Disappointment Deceives* at www.discoveryseries.org/cb041.

FISHING: If you are fishing from a boat, it's not a good idea to go out alone. Take a friend for help in case something unexpected comes up.

25. WISE COUNSEL

"Jesus grew in wisdom and stature, and in favor with God and men."

LUKE 2:52

I'll never forget Jake. His legs seemed too thin and spindly to hold him against the current of the river. His patched and discolored waders looked older than he was. His fishing vest was tattered and held together with safety pins; his ancient hat was battered and sweat-stained; his antiquated fly rod was scarred and taped.

FAST FACT:

One pundit said of fishing: "There he stands, draped in more equipment than a telephone lineman, trying to outwit an organism with a brain no bigger than a breadcrumb, and getting licked in the process."

I watched as he worked his way upstream to a patch of quiet water and began to cast. Then I took notice! He was fishing the same water I had fished earlier in the day, and he was catching trout where I had caught none. Here was a man who could teach me a thing or two. All I had to do was ask.

We gain insight when we listen to those who have gone before and who know more than we do—insight we miss when our pride stands in the way. We're able to learn from others when we humble ourselves and acknowledge how little we know. Willingness to learn is a mark of those who are truly wise.

Consider our Lord as a young boy, "sitting among the teachers, listening to them and asking them questions" (Luke 2:46). Proverbs 1:5 says that the wise "listen and add to their learning." Let's ask questions of those who've spent their lives seeking God's wisdom.

—David Roper

FOLLOW THE COMPASS

Whom do you look to for spiritual advice? Who can you call on for wise counsel?

From the Guidebook: Read Luke 2:46–52.

ICE FISHING: Your guide-line can be kept from freezing if you spray it with non-sticking cooking spray.

26. THE BATTLE IS ON!

" 'Come follow me,' Jesus said, 'and I will make you fishers of men.' "

MATTHEW 4:19

A skilled fly fisherman whips his line back and forth over his head. Then he releases the line and sets the fly-like lure down on the water's surface exactly where he wants it. If he's successful, a big rainbow trout will rise, strike the lure, and the fisherman will set the hook. The battle is on!

FAST FACT:
Recent World Fly Fishing Championship venues: 2015, Bosnia and Herzegovina; 2016, Vail, Colorado.

That's one way to catch fish. Halibut fishermen use another method. They go out on the ocean and drop big baited hooks, sometimes as far down as 125 or 150 feet. When one of those big, flat fish goes for the bait and is hooked, he begins a long ride to the surface.

Jesus told Peter and Andrew to follow Him and He would make them "fishers of men" (Matthew 4:18–19). As followers of Christ today, we too are to be "fishing" for people in our world, using different methods to spread the good news. We are to be telling men and women, family and friends, young and old, about their sin, the love of God, and His offer of salvation through faith in Jesus.

Are you fishing for men? Have you tried different methods to tell others about Christ and the gospel? Have you reached out to your neighborhood and community with the good news? Keep following Jesus, and He'll teach you how to fish.

—DAVID EGNER

FOLLOW THE COMPASS

What method do you feel most comfortable with in telling others about Jesus? Giving a book or tract? Suggesting a Christian activity? Asking questions? What are you doing to learn how to fish better?

From the Guidebook: Matthew 4:18–22

HUNTING: Never store a gun in a hard case with foam padding overnight unless you first place it in a silicone sleeve. Also, make sure you use an electric or canister type dryer in your gun safe.

27. RETURN TO YOUR ROOTS

On Point:
Resisting Satan

*"So then, just as you received Christ Jesus as Lord, continue
to live in him, rooted and built up in him."*

Colossians 2:6–7

It happens every September. The salmon in Lake Michigan migrate up the rivers to the very spot they were conceived. It's amazing to watch these determined fish fight their way upstream mile after mile. They swim against strong river currents, negotiate logjams, jump over dams, and dodge fishing lures like mine until they finally arrive where it all began for them.

This annual journey not only makes for some awesome fishing but it's also a powerful picture of the importance of returning to your roots. If the salmon don't return, they won't reproduce and will eventually cease to exist. It is absolutely vital to their life. The same can be true of Christians. If we don't come back to our roots, we will forget what is really true about us and will lose our effectiveness.

FAST FACT:
The average weight of a grown king salmon is 30 to 40 pounds.

We have an enemy who wants to devour us (1 Peter 5:8), and returning to our spiritual roots is an essential part of guarding our hearts (Proverbs 4:23) from him. At the very moment we accept Christ as our Savior, God gives us a new covenant heart (Ezekiel 36:26–27). We become new creations in Christ (2 Corinthians 5:17). Sin may define *how* we act at times, but it no longer defines *who* we truly are. Our truest identity is rooted in Jesus Christ.

Our true hearts are now one with Christ and therefore good. It is vitally important that we come back to this truth over and over because Satan will try everything he can to make us feel defeated. We need to resist him by returning to our roots.

—JEFF OLSON

FOLLOW THE COMPASS

Who benefits the most if you were to believe that you are rotten to the core? How do you really view your heart? Does it harmonize with what the Bible teaches about the new heart you gained when you became a "new creation"?

From the Guidebook: Read Philippians 1:6.

FISHING: Want to catch larger fish? Professional anglers often use larger baits when targeting extremely large fish. By using big stick baits or large soft plastic lures, anglers can increase their chances of catching big fish that are looking for a good meal and decrease the chances of catching smaller fish.

28. LET'S GO FISHING!

"[Jesus] said to them, 'Come with me by yourselves to a quiet place and get some rest.'"

MARK 6:31

Philipp Melancthon, the great Reformation theologian, once said to his friend Martin Luther, "This day you and I will discuss the governance of the universe." What Luther said in response was unexpected: "This day you and I will go fishing and leave the governance of the universe to God."

Dr. M. R. De Haan, the founder of Radio Bible Class (now RBC Ministries), always carried the responsibility of leadership with a conscientious seriousness of purpose. His ministry of speaking, writing, and broadcasting touched the lives of millions. Yet he also loved taking time out to "wet a line," and he did it often enough to balance out the responsibilities of his work. Over the years, Dr. De Haan's fishing excursions took him to Florida, to Puget Sound, to Michigan's Upper Peninsula, and to Canada.

If we are going to serve Christ effectively, we need balance in our lives. We cannot go full speed in the work of the Lord for too long without rest or diversion. We have to counterbalance the seriousness of our mission with good relaxation.

FAST FACT:

On September 27, 2008, President George W. Bush signed a document that ensures that fishing continues to take place on government lands. He said he signed it "to recognize the value of recreational fishing as a sustainable activity in federal waters."

It's important to be diligent in our work for the Lord. But sometimes we get so engrossed in our tasks and activities that we become exhausted and begin to lose perspective. We need to rest, as our Lord advised the disciples. We just may have to say, "Let's go fishing!"

—DAVID EGNER

FOLLOW THE COMPASS

What are you doing this week to set aside some recreational, renewal time? Could going fishing be a part of that holy endeavor?

From the Guidebook: Read Mark 6:7–13, 30–31.

FISHING: You can make your fishing lures stand out at night by adding a couple dots of glow-in-the dark paint or by spraying them with fishing spray that gives off ultraviolet light.

29. THE ART OF MAN FISHING

*"Immediately they left the boat and
their father and followed him. "*
MATTHEW 4:22

Thomas Boston, a young minister and fly fisherman from Scotland, wrote this in his diary in 1699: "Reading in secret, my heart was touched with Matthew 4:19, 'Follow Me, and I will make you fishers of men.' My soul cried out for the accomplishing of that to me, and I was very desirous to know how I might follow Christ, so as to be a fisher of men."

Boston later wrote a booklet titled, *A Soliloquy on the Art of Man Fishing*, in which he spelled out what he learned about soul winning by following the Master Angler. He pointed out that the habits of fish and the habits of sinners are often quite similar.

FAST FACT:
Loch Lomond, the largest loch in Scotland, is a fly fisherman's paradise.

I am an avid fisherman, and I have worked our Idaho trout streams many times. I agree with Boston that catching fish and winning souls are very much alike. But analogy can only take us so far. The best way to become an effective "fisher of men" is simply to follow Jesus—which is what Andrew, Simon, James, and John were all implored to do in Matthew 4.

For us following Jesus means watching how the Master "fished" and then imitating Him. It involves reading the Scriptures and lingering over His words and deeds, learning how He "caught souls." Then we must cry out, as Thomas Boston did, and ask Jesus to make us like Him—great "fishers of men."

—DAVID ROPER

FOLLOW THE COMPASS

Jesus told His new disciples, "Follow me." What does it mean to you to follow Jesus in a way that helps you learn from Him?

From the Guidebook: Read Matthew 4:18–22

FISHING: Don't be afraid to try different lure colors until you find a color that the fish will hit.

30. DEAD DUCKS DON'T FLUTTER

On Point:
Handling life's struggles

"What I want to do I do not do, but what I hate I do."

ROMANS 7:15

Many years ago, a wealthy man went duck hunting with a hired hand named Sam. They took a horse and carriage, and along the way a rim came off one of the wheels. As Sam hammered it back on, he accidentally hit his finger. Instantly he let go with some bad words. He quickly fell to his knees, asking God's forgiveness. "Lord, it's so difficult at times to live the Christian life," he prayed.

"Sam," said the man, "I know you're a Christian, but tell me why you struggle so. I'm an atheist, and I don't have problems like that."

Sam didn't know what to say. Just then two ducks flew overhead. The man raised his gun and two shots rang out. "Leave the dead one and go after that wounded bird!" he shouted. Sam pointed at the duck that was fluttering desperately to escape and said, "I've got an answer for you now, Boss. You said that my Christianity isn't any good because I have to struggle so. Well, I'm the wounded duck, and I struggle to get away from the devil. But Boss, you're the dead duck!"

FAST FACT:
Duck-hunting expert Jeff Matura suggests three duck-calling tips: Buy a quality call, sound like a real duck (this takes practice), and adapt your call to the right bird and the right situation.

That insight fits Paul's description of his Christian experience in Romans 7:14–25. Struggle is one evidence of God's work in our lives. Forgiveness of sin is available, so don't despair. Remember, dead ducks don't flutter.

—Dennis De Haan

FOLLOW THE COMPASS

Do you feel that you are struggling in your Christian life? Do you see that the struggle is a good sign? In what ways?

From the Guidebook: Read Romans 7:14–25.

HUNTING: When you're shooting at an animal—aim small so that you miss small.

31. POWER DRIVEN

"Whoever wants to be great among you must become your servant, and whoever wants to be first must be your slave—just as the Son of Man did not come to be served, but to serve, and to give his life as a ransom for many."

MATTHEW 20:26–28

We are often attracted by power. Tournament fishermen need more powerful motors to get to the best spots most quickly. Bow hunters want the fastest bows. We are intrigued by vehicles that have more horsepower.

FAST FACT:

Want power? The newer top-of-the line DFI (Direct Fuel Injected) outboard motors offer power, fuel efficiency, and are usually quieter than other motors.

In life, many of us are power driven. We are "take control" type of people. We get things done! Sometimes our drivenness has a price tag —it can alienate us from people and may even damage or destroy relationships, but we get jobs done!

Jesus was a model of power. It's hard to comprehend how He could just speak and calm a storm. And not only stop the storm but also calm the sea!

But when it came to relating to people, Jesus shifted into a different mode. He humbled Himself and became a servant! His focus was on others—accepting them, encouraging them, equipping them to accomplish a task bigger than they could comprehend.

Jesus expects us to serve others. How much are we trying to control others (spouse, children, friends, fellow workers) or are we really serving them? Let us encourage, promote, and help others succeed in following Christ.

—MAURY DE YOUNG

FOLLOW THE COMPASS

Make a list of some of the people who are close to you. Honestly reflect on how much you are trying to control them instead of trying to serve each person you know.

From the Guidebook: Read Mark 4

FISHING: Take a motion sickness pill if you are going fishing on the ocean or on one of the Great Lakes.

32. LOVE IS SPELLED T-I-M-E

"Train a child in the way he should go, and when he is old he will not turn from it."

PROVERBS 22:6

I'll never forget the first time my dad took me deer hunting with him. I was only five years old and had a tendency to be quite active. Because I had a difficult time sitting still, I often spooked deer before Dad could get his sights on them. In spite of my being a deer hunting liability, Dad continued to take me along on his hunts. We were buddies, and he felt it was more important to spend time with me than kill a deer.

Though over 50 years have passed, I often find myself thinking of the incredible memories we made as a father and son in a deer woods. I didn't realize it at the time, but many of the experiences we shared helped lay the foundation for a successful career as a wildlife photographer and white-tailed deer researcher. But more importantly, our time in the out-of-doors introduced me to the God of all creation.

FAST FACT:

In 37 states, there is no minimum age for hunting. The most restrictive state is Rhode Island, where the minimum age is 15.

Unfortunately, fathers today spend little time with their sons and daughters. All too often the challenge of hunting big-racked whitetail bucks keeps dads from including their children in their hunts, for fear they'll miss that once-in-a-lifetime trophy. In doing so, they rob themselves of the joys of bonding and sharing the wonders of God's creation with their children.

Had my father not shared nature with me at such an early age, there is a strong possibility I would not know Jesus as my personal Savior today.

—CHARLES ALSHEIMER

FOLLOW THE COMPASS

If you are a parent, how do you think you are doing in the "spending time with your kids" category? Should you set aside some time in the next week just to hang out with your children? Plan accordingly.

From the Guidebook: Read Proverbs 4:10-19.

HUNTING: Always hunt down wind of a big game animal or they will smell you like a pair of dirty socks.

33. FACE YOUR GIANTS

*"As the Philistine moved closer to attack him,
David ran quickly toward the battle line to meet him.
Reaching into his bag and taking out a stone, he
slung it and struck the Philistine on the forehead."*

1 Samuel 17:48–49

I've been facing giants my entire life. I spent a lot of my life recovering from leg and hip operations that resulted from being born with cerebral palsy. Every time I went under the knife, I had to be strong and courageous, despite my young age. My physical problems were my giant, and I had little hope of ever overcoming them.

FAST FACT:
Tracy Breen is a full-time outdoor writer and seminar speaker. To learn more about Tracy, visit his Web site at www.tracybreen.com.

As an adult, I continue to face giants; but they are different now. I still experience physical pain. Operations are again on the horizon. However, the biggest giant I faced was the fear of speaking in front of others. Speaking in front of others isn't the same as standing in front of an actual giant like David did, but to most of us, a crowd of people can seem bigger than an actual giant!

Can you imagine being David and trusting God while walking out in the open against such a fierce competitor with nothing more than a rock and a slingshot in your hand? Trusting God proved to be beneficial for David and his people. He killed the giant and changed the course of history.

The first time I spoke at a game dinner, I talked about harvesting big game on a budget and shared my testimony. As I looked out over the crowd, I trembled with fear. Eventually, my knowledge on the subject and sense of humor went into overdrive and everything went well. Speaking to large crowds of men and women about Christ and about hunting is one of the most important things I do. If I hadn't faced my giant, I would have missed out on the blessing that speaking to others has brought into my life.

Facing your giants, whatever they are, can be tough. Trusting God when the giant in front of us seems so real and intimidating can really stretch our faith. However, by throwing the stone and defeating our giants, we learn to trust God and realize that we can face any giant as long as Christ is by our side.

—Tracy Breen

FOLLOW THE COMPASS

Have you faced your giants and conquered them? Looking back, did it give you more confidence in yourself? Did it strengthen your relationship with Christ?

For Further Reading: Read *Facing Your Giants* by Max Lucado.

HUNTING: Never shoot a gun unless you are certain you have the right ammunition for that gun. Check the barrel for ammunition type, and make sure your ammo box matches that information.

34. RUN FOR COVER

*"Rescue me from my enemies, O Lord,
for I hide myself in you."*

PSALM 143:9

FAST FACT:
Chinook salmon are the largest Pacific salmon, sometimes weighing in at more than 100 pounds.

At daybreak we were already trolling on Puget Sound. The herring were plentiful, and all the fish were hungry. By 7:30 I had landed three beautiful silver salmon and enjoyed several other strikes. Then suddenly they stopped biting. Scores of others in boats nearby started their motors and headed for shore. Bert, my fishing partner, spoke up, "We might as well go in too. It's all over for today." Pointing to the right, he concluded, "There they come, the 'killer whales'!"

Advancing on a wide front, their black fins cutting the water and their blowing now plainly audible, they moved across the bay. Almost every boat made for shore—not because they were afraid of the intruders, but because the fish had vanished! The moment the "killers" made their appearance, the salmon fled to the safety of the rocks and the vegetation at the bottom. Wise fish! They saw death coming and therefore made all haste to find shelter.

In Numbers 35:9–15, we read that God had appointed six towns to be known as "cities of refuge," to which a person could flee when pursued by an avenger. Once inside the area, he was safe. From this we learn an important lesson, expressed by David in Psalm 143:9. Seeking deliverance, he exclaims, "I hide myself in You!" He recognized the enemy overtaking him and ran for refuge to the Savior. As the salmon seeks a hiding place when he sees danger approaching, we too must find shelter from the coming judgment. There is only one place of safety—it is in Christ! Do not delay. Turn to Him now in faith and be saved.

—M. R. DE HAAN

FOLLOW THE COMPASS

When was the last time you ran to the Savior for refuge? Do you often look for other places for rescue instead of to God? How can you change that pattern?

From the Guidebook: Read Numbers 35:9–15

HUNTER SAFETY: Be sure of your target and what lies in front of and beyond your target.

35. FOUR FISHING TIPS

*"[Simon and Andrew] were casting a net into the lake,
for they were fishermen."*

MATTHEW 4:18

In his book *The Uttermost Star,* F. W. Boreham quoted a rhyme that gives four tips on how to catch fish.

Be sure your face is toward the light;
Study the fish's curious ways;
Then keep yourself well out of sight,
And cherish patience all your days.

FAST FACT:

One habit of yellow perch that comes in handy is that they are relatively quiet at night, which means it's best to fish for them in daylight hours.

Boreham then applied the poem, line by line, to a Christian fishing for men. He wrote, "Be sure your face is toward the light. The skillful angler will always be careful to see that the sun shines upon his face and that his shadow falls behind him. . . . The only man who can hopefully angle for fish or for [people] is he of the radiant face, he of the shadow unseen!

"Study the fish's curious ways." Let no one think that it's possible to become a successful angler by learning all about lines and hooks and rods and reels! The learner must study fish and must know the things that please them, the things that repel them. . . . The one who would catch people must understand people!

"Then keep yourself well out of sight." No one ever yet secured large catches, either of fish or of people, who was fond of thrusting himself or herself into inordinate prominence!

"And cherish patience all your days." There will be times when you will have to wait for long, long periods without so much as a nibble; and you will be tempted to give it all up! . . . [but the person who is patient] will enjoy the unspeakable rapture of the fisherman's triumph at the last!"

When Jesus started gathering people to be His disciples— His fishers of men—He began with real fishermen. They knew the tricks of the trade? Do you?

—Richard De Haan

FOLLOW THE COMPASS

Which of the four characteristics of fishing make the most sense to you as a fisher of people? Which can you begin to use to influence someone for Jesus?

From the Guidebook: Read Matthew 4:18–22.

FISHING: Freshwater fish tend to bite best on cloudy days.

36. PERFECT? OR FAR FROM IT?

*"If we claim to be without sin, we deceive
ourselves and the truth is not in us."*

1 JOHN 1:8

In his book *Helping Those Who Don't Want Help*, Marshall Shelley told of a pastor who was backing out of his garage when he heard a "snap." His favorite fishing pole was now in two pieces.

"Who was using my fishing pole?" he asked.

"I was, Dad," said his five-year-old son. "I was playing with it and set it against the garage door. I forgot to put it away."

The pastor wasn't pleased, but he said to his son, "Well, thank you for telling me," and went on his way. Two days later, the boy was shopping with his mother. He said, "Mom, I've got to buy Dad a new fishing pole. I broke his other one. Here's my money." And he handed her his total life savings—two dollars.

FAST FACT:
Fly-fishing rods range from 7 feet to 16 feet in length, but the most common is the 10-footer.

"You don't have to do that," said his mother. "But I want to, Mom," came the reply. "I found out that Dad loves me more than he loves his fishing pole." As the pastor told his congregation about the incident, he commented, "When I heard that, I felt great. I felt that for once I had done something right."

After the service, several men told the pastor, "I appreciate your saying, 'For once I did something right.' I thought pastors always did everything right." By saying what he did, their pastor was admitting that he too struggled with doing right. And this encouraged them.

We're wrong to think we must always appear to be "on top of it." We need not reveal all our faults and failures, but when we learn to be open and real, especially as leaders, people will be helped by what we say.

—DAVID EGNER

FOLLOW THE COMPASS

Do you ever have a hard time admitting that you are wrong? Why is that? Is there anything in 1 John 1:8 that speaks to you and helps you see why, in that regard, you are, well, wrong?

From the Guidebook: Read James 5:13–20.

HUNTING: Hunt in rubber boots. Leather boots retain smells that animals will pick up on.

37. HAVING A MIND TO WORK

*"So we rebuilt the wall till all of it reached half its height,
for the people worked with all their heart."*

NEHEMIAH 4:6

Nehemiah's remarkable success in rebuilding the walls of Jerusalem can be largely credited to the industrious attitude of his helpers. The Bible says that they "worked with all their heart." Because they gave themselves wholeheartedly to the task at hand, they accomplished outstanding results.

A poor, hungry young man stood idly on a bridge watching some fishermen. Seeing one of them with a basket full of fish by his side, he said, "If I had a catch like that, I'd be happy. I'd sell it and buy some food and clothes." "I'll give you that many fish if you do a small favor for me," said the fisherman. "What do you want me to do?" came the reply. "Just tend this line awhile. I've got some business down the street." Gladly the young man accepted the offer. After the man left, the trout and bass continued snapping greedily at the baited hook. Soon he lost all his depression in the excitement of pulling in a large number of fish. When the angler returned, he said to the young man, "I'll keep my promise to you by giving you everything you've caught. And I hope you've learned a lesson. You mustn't waste time daydreaming and merely wishing for things. Instead, get busy and cast in a line for yourself!"

FAST FACT:
You know the saying: "Give a man a fish and he has food for a day; teach him how to fish, and you can get rid of him for the entire weekend."

Examine your attitude toward your job. A wholehearted approach to any task is most important. Don't be a clock-watcher. Display an enthusiasm that indicates you want to work "with all your heart."

—HENRY BOSCH

FOLLOW THE COMPASS

Love your job? Hate your job? What makes the difference in how you view your work?

From the Guidebook: Read Nehemiah 4:1–6.

FISH: If a fish has swallowed the hook, you can still release it back into the water after cutting the line. The hook will eventually dissolve, and the fish should survive.

38. AIM FOR THE HEART

"Above all else, guard your heart."
PROVERBS 4:23

The knock on the door came at 2:30 in the morning. A car had just hit a deer in front of my brother's house and severely injured it. The police were informing him they were going to put the animal down.

The deer was an eight-point buck, still in velvet. He was alive, but obviously suffering. The humane thing would be to put the animal down.

The police officer, who apparently wasn't a hunter, fired a shot into the body of the deer, but it didn't do the job. So he fired a second shot and immediately a third. Surprisingly, the deer was still alive, so my brother piped up and suggested, "It might work better if you shoot it in the heart." Thankfully, the officer took his advice and the fourth round did the trick.

FAST FACT:
The average deer shot in the vitals will go no more than 100 yards.

Any good hunter knows the best shot placement for a quick kill is in the vital organs. An animal doesn't last long after suffering a fatal wound to the chest cavity.

Figuratively speaking, it's the same way with people. We don't function well after suffering a personal blow to the heart. Whether it's self-inflicted because of our sin or caused by the sins of others, the wound can absolutely level us. It can take us out for days or weeks or months. Sometimes it can wipe us out for years.

That is why in Proverbs the Bible exhorts us, "Above all else, guard your heart, for it is the wellspring of life" (Proverbs 4:23).

—Jeff Olson

FOLLOW THE COMPASS

How are you guarding your heart? What threatens your heart for God the most?

From the Guidebook: Read Proverbs 4:20–27.

HUNTER SAFETY: When hunting turkeys, don't wear anything red, blue, or black. They might lead a hunter to mistake you for a turkey, which has those colors.

39. THE BLOWFISH SYNDROME

"Do nothing out of selfish ambition or vain conceit, but in humility consider others better than yourselves."

PHILIPPIANS 2:3

Some fishermen are familiar with the aquatic creature called the blowfish. It has no particular value to the one who catches it—except that it may help to cultivate the angler's patience, for it often seizes bait intended for better fish. Also, the blowfish is unattractive; it has a large mouth and a wrinkled body that looks like worn-out leather. When you turn it over and tickle it, the flabby fish puffs up until it is swollen like a globe.

FAST FACT:
Puffer fish are cute, but they are better left in the tank or in the water. They are poisonous—not to the touch, but if eaten.

People can be like that. A little flattery, a little tickling of their vanity, and they swell up—giving the semblance of greatness. Pride inflates them, and they puff up like the blowfish. But there's nothing substantial about them; they are all air.

This condition takes other forms with more serious consequences. For example, the Christians to whom Paul wrote in 1 Corinthians 5 were tolerating immorality. Instead of being grieved over sin in their midst, they were actually "puffed up" (1 Corinthians 5:2). Here was a sure sign of carnality and immaturity—they were proud when they should have been mourning. How tragic! God desires that we should be "built up" in Christ—never "puffed up" with pride.

What should be the continual attitude of God's children? Notice what Paul said in Philippians 2. "Do nothing out of selfish ambition or vain conceit, but in humility consider others better than yourselves" (v. 3). If we take this seriously, we won't have the characteristics of the puffed-up blowfish.

—PAUL VAN GORDER

FOLLOW THE COMPASS

How does pride affect your life? What irritates you in people who are overly proud?

From the Guidebook: Read Philippians 2:1–8.

HUNTING: To make sure your shoes aren't a problem in alerting deer, wear dark-soled boots. Otherwise, if you are sitting, the animal might see your boots before it sees you.

40. WISHES AND HOPES

*"Delight yourself also in the Lord and he will
give you the desires of your heart."*

PSALM 37:4

A certain airline pilot had a peculiar habit. Whenever he took off from his hometown of Minneapolis, he would ask the copilot to take the controls. Then he would stare intently out the window for a few moments.

Finally the copilot's curiosity got the best of him, so he asked, "What do you always look at down there?"

FAST FACT:

Minnesota has more than 5,600 lakes, ponds, reservoirs, and other bodies of water available for fishing.

"See that boy fishing on that riverbank?" the pilot asked. "I used to fish from that same spot when I was a kid. Whenever a plane flew over, I would watch it until it disappeared and wish that I could be the pilot." With a sigh he added, "Now I wish I could be back down there fishing."

It's natural to spend time thinking about where we'd like to be or what we'd like to have. But we must evaluate our desires to make sure they are consistent with what God says will truly satisfy.

King David found satisfaction by putting first things first. His joy was rooted in the strength of the Lord and the salvation He provided (Psalm 21:1–2). It was because David sought the Lord that God gave him the desires of his heart (37:4).

When our desires conform to God's will, we're not likely to waste time wishing for things that can't satisfy. Real joy comes not in getting what we want, but in wanting to be close to God.

—David Egner

FOLLOW THE COMPASS

Have you ever thought about what Psalm 37:4 means when it says "the desires of your heart"? What does it tell you about your desires if you delight in the Lord? What kinds of desires will those be?

From the Guidebook: Read Psalm 21:1–7.

PUPPY TRAINING: When getting a new puppy for hunting, let him sleep in the same kennel that you will use to transport him in your vehicle (if that is possible). He will adjust to travel more easily if he is in comfortable and familiar quarters.

41. SAVE THE PEOPLE!

*"Then they will go away to eternal punishment,
but the righteous to eternal life."*

MATTHEW 25:46

Careless hunting practices and the destruction of natural habitats have wiped some of God's creatures off the face of the earth. A "Save the Whales" bumper sticker put it in grim perspective. Beside a picture of a whale were just three words, "Extinction is forever."

FAST FACT:

One of the weirdest extinct creatures is the Quagga, an African mammal that had zebra-type stripes on half its brown body but no stripes on the other half. It became extinct in the 1880s.

That's a sobering thought—one that has caused people around the world to mobilize and do all they can to save the whales. If we were to kill them off, they would never exist again. For anyone interested in animals, that's a grave prospect.

There's a certain irony to this understand-able concern for animals. While we spend millions of dollars and hours of time to ensure their continued existence, we often fail to do anything about the eternal destiny of people. Yet for those who reject Jesus, there is a future that is worse than extinction—"everlasting punishment" (Matthew 25:46) in "eternal fire prepared for the devil and his angels" (v. 41).

It is sad that some animals, such as the passenger pigeon and the Labrador duck, have become extinct. But how much more we should be concerned for people! They have a choice—

to live with God in eternal joy or to suffer with the devil in the lake of fire. In our concern for God's creatures, let's not forget the human ones, the ones for whom Christ died.

—DAVE BRANON

FOLLOW THE COMPASS

Is there anyone you are concerned about because you are not sure of his or her salvation? What plan do you have for helping to introduce this person to the gospel?

From the Guidebook: Read Matthew 25:31–46.

HUNTING SAFETY: Make sure you know all the laws relating to the wildlife you are hunting, and if you see violations turn in the violators.

42. MORE THAN FISHING

"Come, follow me . . . and I will make you fishers of men."
MATTHEW 4:19

Henry Thoreau once said, "Many men go fishing all of their lives without knowing that it is not fish they are after." Thoreau was on to something. There is *more* to it than the thrill of reeling in a big fish. Beneath our desire to fish is a deeper God-given desire for adventure.

In his excellent book *Wild at Heart*, John Eldredge points out that Adam was created in the wilderness, outside of the Garden of Eden. Genesis 2 tells us God first created Adam and then He placed him in the garden He had planted (Genesis 2:7-8).

FAST FACT:

More Americans fish (40 million) than play golf (24.4 million) and tennis (10.4 million) combined.

Adam was created in an untamed environment, and ever since then men have longed to get out into activities that are challenging and risky. That's one reason so many keep searching for tastes of adventure in a recreational activity like fishing. The problem is that fishing is as far as the adventure often goes for many men. It tends to stop there, and it's not enough. It's too little of an adventure. God made them to be a part of a much greater adventure.

There is no greater adventure in this life than to follow the God of the universe. The stories of the Bible show that when God calls people out to follow Him, their lives are crawling with adventure. For example, God called Abraham to leave behind all he was familiar with and to follow Him into unknown territory (Genesis 12:1). No map or GPS—just God and the open wilderness.

True adventure begins when we follow God!

—JEFF OLSON

FOLLOW THE COMPASS

What deeper adventure is God calling you into?

For Further Study: Check out the book *Wild at Heart* by John Eldredge (Thomas Nelson, 2001).

HUNTING: Don't lose your stand. Make a map of the area in which you have your treestand—or even somehow mark a path to it and away from it.

43. "YOU DID JUST FINE"

"There is no fear in love. But perfect love drives out fear."
1 JOHN 4:18

In his book *Winning Through Caring*, Matthew Prince told the following story: "A rugged mountain man from Tennessee was big-game hunting in Alaska when he and his guide were charged by a bear. As the guide began firing, the man froze. The guide's rifle ran out of bullets. The bear was still charging, so the guide wrenched the rifle from his guest's hands and continued shooting. As the huge animal dropped a few feet from the men, the mountaineer began to apologize profusely. His guide said, 'Don't feel bad. You did just fine.' That honest mountain man said, 'What do you mean "fine"? I froze on you. I was no help at all.' The guide responded, 'No, you did just fine. Most of the tourists run off with their rifles!'"

FAST FACT:

Want to go bear hunting in Alaska? It'll most likely cost you at least $10,000 for a guide, transportation, and equipment.

Does this describe the feeling you have when you think of witnessing for Christ? Perhaps you've been a Christian for years, but you've never really told anyone about Him. You want to speak out for the Lord, but you have a paralyzing fear of what might happen. I want to encourage you. One of the most important elements in becoming a witnessing Christian is having the desire to witness. Therefore, like the frightened hunter, so far you are doing just fine.

Now you need to go one step further and put desire into action. Write a letter of personal testimony to a friend or loved one. Invite your neighbor over for coffee and tell him or her about Christ. Speak to the person at work who runs the machine next to yours. Let your love overcome your fear, and you'll discover that you did just fine!

—DAVID EGNER

FOLLOW THE COMPASS

What are you afraid of? Could your love for another person conquer your fear of telling that person what he or she needs to hear from you?

From the Guidebook: Read Matthew 28:16–20.

HUNTING: If you will be hunting in freezing weather, take WD-40 to spray on your gun's pump action so it doesn't freeze up.

44. LEAVE THE DOG AT HOME!

"Clothe yourselves with the Lord Jesus Christ, and do not think about how to gratify the desires of the sinful nature."

ROMANS 13:14

The story is told of a man who liked to hunt pheasants. He thought he could do better if he had a dog to help him, so he bought one. However, he was disappointed when he discovered that the dog was interested only in chasing rabbits. The man had acquired a hound dog when what he needed was a bird dog. So instead of hunting pheasants, as he really wanted to, the man spent his time doing what his dog preferred. Finally, the hunter decided he had better leave the dog at home.

FAST FACT:

Did you know that there is a National Bird Dog Museum? It is located in Grand Junction, Tennessee. Read about it at www. birddogfoundation. com.

This story reminds me of the apostle Paul's words in Romans 7. He wrote, "For what I want to do I do not do, but what I hate I do" (v. 15). Paul was speaking of the conflict between his old sinful nature, the flesh, and the new nature he received when he was born again. So then, as long as we're governed by the flesh (the law of sin), we'll respond much like the man in today's story. We'll find ourselves doing what we don't want to do and failing to do what we know we should.

The hunter solved his problem by taking decisive action. He equipped himself for pheasant hunting and went out without the distracting dog. That's what we must do in the spiritual realm. As we prepare for each day, let's choose to obey the injunction, "Clothe yourselves with the Lord Jesus Christ, and do not think about how to gratify the desires of the sinful nature." When we yield to Christ, rely on His strength, and put Him first, we will reject the evil impulses that arise from the law of sin in our members. That's how we "leave the dog at home."

—RICHARD DE HAAN

FOLLOW THE COMPASS

Do you have any "dogs" in your life that you should leave at home? How does Romans 13:14 help you to do that?

From the Guidebook: Read Ephesians 4:17–32.

HUNTING: Bird hunting without a dog? Take a fishing rod and reel with you to hook the fallen duck.

45. WORLDLY WEIGHTS

"Therefore, since we are surrounded by such a great cloud of witnesses, let us throw off everything that hinders and the sin that so easily entangles, and let us run with perseverance the race marked out for us."

HEBREWS 12:1

About 10 years after he was converted, an Indonesian believer discovered that his hunting bow was affecting his spiritual life. He had purchased it to shoot game, but his excursions into the woods were becoming so enjoyable that he became lax in church attendance. Then one day someone wronged him. He felt a strong urge to settle the score with his bow and arrow just as he would have done before he was a Christian. But immediately he recognized that this reaction was an evidence of spiritual decline in his life. So he took his weapon to an outdoor service, and in the presence of fellow Christians he broke it in pieces and threw them on a pile of wood for burning. His bow and arrow had become a spiritual weight that had to be given up—a problem Hebrews 12:1 addresses.

FAST FACT:

One way to use your love of outdoors activities for godly purposes is to help sponsor a sportsman's dinner. Groups such as Sportspersons Ministries International (www.spi-int.org) can help you find out how.

Maybe your fishing equipment, your golf clubs, your motorhome, your television set, or your lakeside cottage is keeping you from going to church faithfully or serving the Lord as you should. If so, do something about it. You may have to get rid of whatever is coming between you and the Lord. On the other hand, it may not be necessary to give up these things, but you do have to make an adjustment in your lifestyle. In either case, act decisively and "lay aside every weight."

—Herb Vander Lugt

FOLLOW THE COMPASS

Would you say that there is any recreation or other leisure activity that keeps you from your walk with the Lord? What might be some measures you can take to correct that misalignment of priorities?

From the Guidebook: Read Hebrews 12:1–6.

HUNTING: If you use a tree stand, do not carry your gear into the stand with you. Instead, use a haul line to get your gear into and out of the tree.

46. FISH HARD

" 'Follow me,' Jesus said, 'and I will make you fishers of men.' "

MARK 1:17

Okay, I admit it. I like to fish. No, I'm not the buy-the-latest-bass-boat, get-out-every-weekend kind of guy. But I enjoy fishing for walleyes at a nearby dam in the summer or catching perch through the ice on one of Michigan's many lakes in winter.

That makes me interested in things related to fishing. So I was hooked when I saw this bumper sticker on the back of an old pickup truck:

"Life's Short: Fish Hard."

I chuckled, but the more I thought about it the more I was caught by this idea: As a follower of Jesus Christ, I am a "fisher of men." I have been commanded by the Lord Jesus to proclaim the gospel message (Matthew 28:19–20), to tell others about the wonderful, saving love of God for all people.

I thought too about the statement, "Life's short." It is! How quickly 10, 20, 30 years pass. All too soon our children are starting school, graduating, marrying, having children of their own. All too quickly those friends and family members we always wanted to talk to about Jesus Christ are no longer with us.

FAST FACT:
Here's another saying: "The only certainty in fishing is that there is no certainty."

Yes, life is short. So, as obedient followers of Jesus Christ, let's "fish hard" to bring others to Him.

—David Egner

FOLLOW THE COMPASS

How fast does life seem to be going for you? Does that mean you should have some goals in the area of "fishing hard" for souls?

From the Guidebook: Read Mark 1:14–20.

ICE FISHING: Take along a mechanics magnet. Then, if you drop something metallic through the ice fishing hole, you might be able to retrieve it with the magnet.

47. THE GREAT IMPOSTOR

"Put on the full armor of God so that you can take your stand against the devil's schemes."

EPHESIANS 6:11

The Arctic polar bear feeds almost entirely on seals. To enjoy such a meal, he sometimes resorts to a cunning bit of trickery. If the hole in the ice through which the seal gets his food is not too far from the edge of open water, the polar bear will take a deep breath, slip underwater, and swim to the seal's fishing hole. He will then imitate a fish by scratching lightly on the underside of the ice. When the seal hears this sound, he dives in for a quick supper, only to find himself suddenly caught in the huge, hungry embrace of his predator.

FAST FACT:

According to some estimates, there are somewhere around 25,000 polar bears in existence worldwide.

The devil entices us in a similar way. He baits us with some seemingly harmless pleasure and disguises the ugliness of sin with something that looks or sounds appealing. Then, when we've succumbed to the temptation, he catches us in his trap.

Christians have no excuse for being taken in by the deception of the enemy. We can put on the armor of God and with the "shield of faith . . . extinguish all the flaming arrows of the evil one" (Ephesians 6:16).

As we meditate on the truths of God's Word and rely on the Holy Spirit, we can know the difference between what is truly satisfying and what only appears to be. Don't let the great impostor fool you!

—Mart De Haan

FOLLOW THE COMPASS

What armor do you feel that you have on? What pieces are missing? Is there anything else you think you could do to protect yourself from the enemy?

Go Deep: Read Ephesians 6:10–20.

ICE FISHING: If you use minnows for bait, put the hook through their little tails. This results in more action underwater and more attention from the fish.

48. TOO WEAK TO FIGHT?

"Be merciful to me, Lord, for I am faint. . . . Turn, O Lord, and deliver me; save me because of your unfailing love."

PSALM 6:2, 4

Like parents who give special attention to a weak, helpless child, so the Father in heaven is pleased to provide for those who cry out to Him in time of trouble. The Bible speaks of many "heroes of faith" who were thus accorded God's aid (Hebrews 11:32–34). The vacuum of their weakness drew forth His strengthening power, giving them unexpected victory.

FAST FACT:

A white-tailed deer can escape most prey because of two factors: It can run around 30 miles an hour, and it can leap obstacles such as a fence with its hurdling ability.

In speaking of this truth, Dr. A. C. Dixon related the following incident: "A friend of mine who was very fond of hunting lived in an area that abounded with wild deer. One morning as he was walking across the meadows, he heard the baying of hounds in the distance. As they approached, he saw the object of the chase—a young doe, very weary, its tongue hanging out, and panting with exhaustion. Hesitating for a moment and gazing about in a pathetic and frightened manner, the animal saw its pursuers closing in. Its first impulse was to run again, but instead, it fell defenseless at the feet of my friend. He said, 'I stood there for some time with a stick in my hand, fighting off the barking dogs. I was determined that none of them should capture the little deer which in its weakness had appealed to my strength!' "

Believer, your cry for help in your hour of distress will also touch the Father's loving heart. With the psalmist you will soon be able to testify that "the Lord has heard my weeping" (Psalm 6:8). The things that are driving your soul to the point of spiritual exhaustion will then be overcome as He bares His mighty arm in your defense. He will provide the strength you so sorely need!

—HENRY BOSCH

FOLLOW THE COMPASS

What are the hounds that are after you? How helpful would it be to simply turn over the chase to God, acknowledging your weakness and depending on His strength?

Go Deep: Read Psalm 6.

FISHING: Use darker lures when fishing for bass in clear water. The fish can't see lures that are brightly colored as well as they see the dark ones.

49. DISTRACTED BY A MOUSE

"Demas, because he loved this world, has deserted me."
2 TIMOTHY 4:10

Unless we constantly keep before us the singular goal of honoring the Lord, we can easily be distracted by worldly influences.

I am reminded of a story about a man who bought a new hunting dog. Eager to see how he would perform, he took him out one day, hoping to track down big game. No sooner had they gotten into the woods than the animal picked up the trail of a bear. Excitedly the hunter followed close behind. Then suddenly the dog stopped, sniffed the ground, and headed in a different direction. He had caught the smell of a deer that had crossed the path of the bear. A few moments later he halted again, this time captivated by the scent of a rabbit that had crossed the path of the deer. On and on it went until finally the breathless hunter caught up with his dog, only to find him barking triumphantly down the hole of a field mouse.

FAST FACT:

One kind of bear dog is a Karelian bear dog, a black and white beauty that will hunt down a bear and hold it at bay until the dog's master shows up.

Many new Christians start out with the high resolve of keeping the Savior first in their lives. But it isn't long before their whole attention is diverted to things of temporal importance. One pursuit leads to another until they have strayed far from their original purpose. Apparently this is what happened to one of the apostle Paul's companions, for he wrote to Timothy, "Demas, because he loved this world, has deserted me." If the hunter's dog is a picture of you, stop chasing some insignificant rodent of wealth, power, prestige, or pleasure. Turn from all worldly distractions and dedicate your life anew to the Lord.

—Dennis De Haan

FOLLOW THE COMPASS

What is distracting you in your pursuit of holiness? Is it money? Other people? Recreation? Apathy? Why not ask God to help you to avoid being distracted by these less-important things?

From the Guidebook: Read 1 John 2:12–17.

HUNTING: If you are using a duck decoy in still water, make it look more realistic by using a string that you can pull on occasionally. This creates a ripple in the water, which a real duck would produce.

50. DON'T GET HOOKED

"You belong to your father, the devil, and you want to carry out your father's desire."

JOHN 8:44

It's a quiet spring morning. The mists are still rising as the fisherman glides to his favorite fishing spot. He's after one of those giant bass that hides among the weeds and sunken logs.

Now, this fisherman is probably an honest man who wouldn't cheat on his taxes. But when he's fishing, he's a cunning deceiver. He is out there to snare and to capture. To do that, he's not going to throw a bare hook in the water. That wouldn't fool the fish. So he disguises it with an attractive lure. He may even hide it with that old reliable—the night crawler. He wants the fish to take the bait without noticing the hook. By that time it will be too late. A skilled angler will give just the right jerk and set the hook. And that's the end of the fish's freedom.

FAST FACT:
So, what does a bass want to grab hold of? How about a nice jig and pig?

Satan is also fishing. We are the fish. And the bait is whatever will lure us to take the hook. It usually appeals to a natural desire—such as our need for intimacy or success or security. He uses legitimate needs to hide his real intent, which is to get us to disobey God. He knows that to entice us to take the bait, he has to hide the hook. And he'll make it look as appealing as he can.

Satan is a cunning deceiver. Don't be fooled by his tactics.

—DAVID EGNER

FOLLOW THE COMPASS

Have you had friends who were tricked into following Satan's pathways? What would have helped them avoid getting hooked?

From the Guidebook: Read John 8:31–47.

HUNTING: Use a fawn bleat after deer have been separated (e.g. right after the crops have been harvested or after a deer drive).

51. FISH ON!

"We are more than conquerors through him who loved us."
ROMANS 8:37

"ish on!"

It's a sentence I've shouted many times during the summer while trolling for salmon on Lake Michigan. But this time it was special. The angler who was set to take on this monster was my buddy's 14-year-old son, Jake. Up until that moment, the biggest fish Jake had fought was a small bluegill.

For 25 minutes, Jake battled the fish valiantly. The silver brute made one strong run after another, occasionally shooting out of the water like a missile. As Jake's arms tired from exhaustion, he wondered if the fish would ever quit fighting. Near the end, we even thought the fish got off when it wrapped the line around the boat motor. We almost quit. But then suddenly, the 25-pounder surfaced and within minutes surrendered to our net.

FAST FACT:
A 44-pound Chinook is the largest salmon reeled in from Lake Michigan on the Wisconsin side.

Jake's experience of fighting the salmon captures the ups and downs of our battle against evil. At times, it's exhilarating to join God in His fight against the evil one. We feel alive playing a role in this epic war that started long before the world began. But then there are times we feel so weary from the battle. We can be tempted to believe the lie that we can't go on or that evil has the upper hand.

It is during those discouraging times that we can fight back by *refusing* to believe such lies and *reminding* ourselves of the truth—"in all things we are more than conquerors" through Jesus Christ (Romans 8:37). Standing in the truth doesn't get you out of the fight, but it gets you through it.

—JEFF OLSON

FOLLOW THE COMPASS

Find a new way to remind yourself that you are on the winning team.

From the Guidebook: Read Ephesians 6:14.

FISHING/HUNTING WITH KIDS: There is a cost of taking a child with you. Your mistakes will no longer be private. However, the value of the relationship formed is worth the price.

52. BEWARE OF THE BEAR!

"Like a bear robbed of her cubs, I will attack them."
HOSEA 13:8

If you have visited Alaska, you have no doubt seen warnings about the bears that roam the wilderness. Experienced old-timers who know the habits of bears offer these suggestions for safety:

- Don't climb a tree. Bears climb.
- Don't run. Bears can run faster.
- If the bear is brown, curl up and play dead. If it's black, move wildly and make lots of noise.
- Never, never offer food to a bear.
- Above all, don't get between a mother bear and her cubs.

FAST FACT:
Alaska is home to 100,000 bears, so it is not uncommon for Alaskan residents and visitors to encounter one of the big guys.

In our Bible reading from Hosea, God described himself as being as angry with Israel as a mother bear who has been deprived of her cubs (13:8). God had done so much to show His love, but His people had wandered away from Him and taken the path of disobedience. So He disciplined them, while reminding them of His love (13:4–6; 14:1–9).

We need to learn from what happened to Israel. To avoid God's anger and enjoy His love today:

- Love and worship Him above all (13:4).
- Don't try to hide your sin—confess it (14:1–2).
- Stay on the path of righteousness (14:9).

Our God is a jealous God (Exodus 34:14). He loves us, but He will not tolerate disobedience. Beware of the Bear!

—DAVID EGNER

FOLLOW THE COMPASS

What do you think of the idea that God is jealous? What does that mean to you as you think about other things in life that might attract your attention?

From the Guidebook: Read Hosea 13:1–8.

HUNTING: When you are in an area where bears are prevalent, carry a can of pepper spray with you. Wildlife Specialists in Alaska regularly use pepper spray instead of guns on large bears. When used properly, pepper spray impairs a bear's eyesight and causes short-term breathing problems that quickly discourage an attack.

53. TIGHT LINES

"Always be ready to give an answer to everyone who asks you to give the reason for the hope that you have."

1 PETER 3:15

Fishermen sometimes bestow this blessing on one another: "May you keep a tight line," by which we mean, "May you always have a trout on your line."

As I've gotten older, however, I must confess that a tight line means less to me now than it once did. I get as much enjoyment from fishing as I do from catching.

When I'm fishing, I have more time to walk streamside and enjoy the solitude and silence, and to look for places where fish might be lurking. When I try too hard to catch, I lose too many fish and the enjoyment of the day.

FAST FACT:

Another fishing quote: "The fishing was good; it was the catching that was bad."

—A. K. Best

Jesus calls us to be fishers of men, not catchers (Matthew 4:19). My job is to go where the fish are, walk among them, study their habitat, and learn their ways. And then to toss out a line and see if one rises to the surface. There's more enjoyment in that easy effort, and I have better results.

So I want to fish for people, looking for opportunities to speak a word about Jesus, casting here and there, and leaving the results with God. It's more calming for me and for the "fish"—the folks who might get spooked by my clumsiness.

Thus I now bless my fellow fishers with: "May you keep your line in the water." Or, as another fisherman once put it, "Always be ready" (1 Peter 3:15).

—David Roper

FOLLOW THE COMPASS

Does it help you to know that the decision people make to trust Jesus is between those people and God—and that your responsibility is just to introduce them to the Savior?

From the Guidebook: Read Matthew 4:18–20.

FISHING: Change your monofilament fishing line every year.

54. AIM AT THE TARGET

*"In all your ways acknowledge [the Lord],
and he will make your paths straight."*

PROVERBS 3:6

A group of does came out into the field slightly before the end of shooting hours. As the deer moved out, I chose one for my target. I looked through my scope, centered on the vitals, and gently squeezed the trigger. Several months later we were still enjoying steaks, roasts, and ground venison.

FAST FACT:
Hunting is one of the most effective means we have of managing wildlife in our culture today.

It's important for any big-game hunter to center on the target if he wants to make a good shot. Scopes vary as to what type of reticle, or crosshair, they have, and some even have built-in lines of adjustment for distance. Either way, the hunter still needs to center in on the target.

In life, we need to center in on the target. We need to center our focus on Jesus Christ. The Bible reminds us, "In all your ways acknowledge him, and he will make your paths straight." If we want to live the most satisfying, fulfilled, directed life, our focus needs to be on Jesus Christ.

So often our attention is directed toward everything except our relationship with God. We focus on what is happening, on people, and on problems. It's no wonder we live with so much stress and confusion.

Take time to refocus on the proper target of your life. Set your crosshairs on what God wants in your life, and you will be amazed at how satisfying your life will become.

—MAURY DE YOUNG

FOLLOW THE COMPASS

Reflect on the various areas of your life in a normal day. What adjustments do you need to make to keep Jesus the center of your life?

From the Guidebook: Read Genesis 1:26–28 (When you see the word *rule*, recognize that it means "to manage"); Read Psalm 8 (Note especially vv. 6–8).

HUNTING: To simulate the pressure and increased heart rate that accompanies buck fever, do a few push-ups or run in place for a minute before you practice shooting your rifle or bow. Learning how to concentrate and shoot while tired and out of breath can prepare you for the real moment of truth.

55. THE GIFT

"Be sure to fear the Lord and serve him faithfully with all your heart."

1 Samuel 12:24

I stood motionless in the dark timber, waiting for daylight to arrive. Off in the distance the shrill sound of a bull elk bugling broke the early morning silence. The elk rut was in full swing.

For the next four hours I played cat and mouse with a huge bull as I tried to get within bow range. It was high elk hunting drama at its finest. As my quest to harvest a New Mexico elk unfolded throughout the morning, I was treated to some of the most incredible sights the Rocky Mountains have to offer. It was truly sensory overload!

FAST FACT:

One of the largest New Mexico elks ever taken was a 1,100-pound behemoth with a 7'x 6' frame. The bowhunter who took it down was a Texan named Lacy Harber.

By noon, realizing the bull had won our match, I stopped at the timberline to take in the sights and reflect on the morning. Though I didn't harvest an elk, the show God had treated me to was a blessing beyond measure.

During my lifetime I've had many hunting experiences similar to this elk hunt. Although every hunt has been different, all had a common denominator. What made them all possible is the fact that God created every aspect of those hunts, from me, to the country hunted, to the animals pursued.

God's creation is truly awesome in every way. As you begin this day, take time to thank Him for making it for us to enjoy.

—CHARLES ALSHEIMER

FOLLOW THE COMPASS

What aspect of God's creation stands out in your thinking? What causes awe when you see it and marvel that God spoke it into existence? Have you thanked God today for what He has fashioned on this earth?

From the Guidebook: Read Genesis 1–3.

HUNTING: Don't get discouraged if you use a grunt call and younger bucks run away. This may indicate there is a much larger deer in your area that has been beating up on the younger bucks.

56. LAST-MINUTE SAVE

*" 'For I know the plans I have for you,' declares
the Lord, 'plans to prosper you and not to harm you,
plans to give you hope and a future.' "*

JEREMIAH 29:11

I've hunted all over the United States and Canada for a wide variety of game animals over the last five years. I feel that many of these hunts were orchestrated by God. Some might not believe that God would have His hand in something as unimportant as a hunting trip, but most of the trips have happened because out of the blue, God puts certain individuals in my life. One thing leads to another and before I know it, I am hunting with them or someone they know.

FAST FACT:

In most Western states, the success rate of filling an elk tag with archery gear is around 10 percent.

Because I feel like God's hand is on my hunting trips, I am often amazed when I find myself nearing the end of a hunt and my hunting license has not been filled. I often question why I went on the hunt and why God hasn't presented me with an opportunity to harvest an animal. On some hunts, I go home empty-handed. However, on many hunts God provides me with an opportunity on the very last day of the hunt. I believe that if I would have filled my tag on the first day, the thought of God providing me with an animal might not have crossed my mind. But when it gets down to the wire, we often pray without ceasing in hopes that God will answer our prayers. Hunting is what I do for a living, so being successful at it is important to me. On many occasions, I have prayed for a last-minute opportunity.

In everyday life, God often allows us to be at a spot in life where if we fill the tag, get the job, or survive the life-threatening disease, there is no doubt it happened because of Him. By allowing us to be in a tight spot and rescuing us when it looks like we have no hope of succeeding, we see *His* power, glory, and faithfulness.

—TRACY BREEN

FOLLOW THE COMPASS

Has God ever saved the day for you when your situation looked pretty bleak? Has your faith grown because of it?

From the Guidebook: Read Jeremiah 29.

HUNTING: When turkey hunting, carry a call made by a local call-maker—not a mass-produced call sold at large stores. Often a lovesick gobbler who has been hunted all spring will learn to recognize a hunter's calls. Custom calls often have a different pitch and can fool a call-shy gobbler.

57. FISH IN A TUB

On Point:
Putting a little work into your faith

"Endure hardship with us like a good soldier of Christ Jesus."
2 TIMOTHY 2:3

I read about a man who decided that his weekly fishing excursion was costing him too much money and causing him too much work. Therefore he purchased a large washtub, filled it with water, placed it under a shade tree in his backyard, pulled up a comfortable lawn chair, and started his fishing.

It seemed like a great idea. He thought of the money he was saving and of the fact that he was no longer weary from hooking and unhooking his boat and loading and unloading his motor. He was also avoiding the bother of toting a gasoline can, tackle box, and supply of bait. Often he caught as many fish out of the tub as he did when he worked so hard on the lake or stream! (Exactly none!)

However, this business of fishing in a tub gradually lost its appeal. He never felt the tingle of excitement that comes when the bobber disappears and a sudden tug is felt on the line. He also missed the fact that he no longer could tell stories to his friends about the large fish he caught, or the larger one that got away. Finally, he decided

FAST FACT:

Cost-of-fishing joke: Two guys go on a fishing trip. They spend a fortune on all the equipment. Day 1: Fish all day; nothing; Day 2: Same thing. Day 3: One fish. As they're driving home one says to the other, "Do you realize that this one lousy fish we caught cost us fifteen hundred dollars?" The other guy pauses and says, "Wow! It's a good thing we didn't catch any more!"

that although fishing in a tub is cheaper and easier, it is not nearly as rewarding as going to a lake or stream.

Christians who are primarily concerned with relaxation and ease will soon find that life without discipleship and zealous service is not very rewarding. It's like fishing in a tub! Paul knew this, so he exhorted Timothy to endure hardness like a good soldier, to strive to excel like a determined athlete, and to toil patiently like a faithful farmer. This is the kind of Christian life that pays dividends and produces inner joy and satisfaction.

—HERB VANDER LUGT

FOLLOW THE COMPASS

What kind of hardship have you had to endure while doing the Lord's work? Was it worth the effort?

From the Guidebook: Read 2 Timothy 2:1–10.

HUNTING: Bowhunting in the cold can be tough on the body. Muscles get stiff and ache after sitting in a stand for long hours. To ensure you can get your bow to full draw at the moment of truth, reduce your draw weight by 5 or 10 pounds if you hunt in cold weather.

58. KEEP FOCUSED

*You will keep in perfect peace him whose mind
is steadfast, because he trusts in you.*

ISAIAH 26:3

It wasn't large, but it won the biggest bass and also put me in the winner's category for the most weight. I was fishing a tournament put on by the sportspersons club of our local church. I don't fish many tournaments and don't win many, but on this cold-front "lock jaw" day, I found something that worked.

As I reflected on what made the difference for me, I realized that I had stayed focused. As one nears the end of the tournament and needs another fish or a larger fish, one's tendency is to fish faster to try to cover more territory to find that one hungry bass. At this tournament, I had downsized to a lure that I often use for panfish, and I continued to fish it very slowly. It was hard to wind it in at that speed, as I knew time was running out. But staying focused put a nice bass in the live well and made the difference.

FAST FACT:

Maury is executive director of Sportspersons Ministries International. Find out more about it at www.spi-int.org.

In life, it's hard to stay focused on the right things—particularly as we face more and more stress in our daily lives. But in the midst of the "cold fronts" in life, God has a message for us: He will "keep in perfect peace him whose mind is [focused]" on God.

If we feel restless, confused, afraid, or discouraged, it's time to readjust our focus. Let's stay focused on God and experience the peace that only He can provide.

—MAURY DE YOUNG

GET SERIOUS

Consider which things bother you the most. How much do you focus on them? What result does that bring? Will you attempt to adjust your focus?

From the Guidebook: Read John 14:27 and Colossians 3:15.

FISHING SAFETY: When casting, make sure no one is within range of your flying hook.

59. THE ART OF SELF-SACRIFICE

"I consider my life worth nothing to me, if only I may finish the race and complete the task the Lord Jesus has given me."

ACTS 20:24

I was surprised to learn that in religious art the pelican has long been a symbol of self-sacrifice. While living in Florida and fishing in Gulf Coast waters, I often observed these strange birds, and to me they seemed more like lazy freeloaders than "self-denying saints." With pitiful stares masking hearts full of envy, they would sit at a distance and lust after every fish I caught. And when hungry enough, they would even try to intercept one before I could reel it in.

FAST FACT:

In order to help pelicans become more self-sufficient, Florida outlawed feeding pelicans in 2008. This forces them into the more natural and safer mode of fishing for themselves.

The reason they have a reputation for "holiness," however, doesn't come from their behavior as much as their appearance. If you notice carefully the pelican's huge beak, it looks like the end has been dipped in red dye. A myth has grown up around this scarlet tip. It is said that when a mother pelican cannot find food for her young, she thrusts her beak into her breast and nourishes her little ones with her own blood. The early church saw in this legend a beautiful picture of what Christ did for us and what we in turn should do for one another.

The pelican, then, not only speaks of the Savior, but it is also a picture of us, God's blood-bought children. We as fallen humans are more generally known by our greed than by our self-sacrifice—very unlikely representatives of our Savior. But through faith in Christ's atoning death, we are "marked in red" as being the forgiven and transformed children of God. Therefore, we should no longer be characterized by those traits that reflect our old sinful flesh. Rather, as new creatures in Christ, let us practice the art of self-sacrificing love.

—MART DE HAAN

FOLLOW THE COMPASS

Do you still manifest any traits from your pre-salvation life—habits or thoughts or activities that clearly don't honor God? What's the best way to get rid of those old traits?

From the Guidebook: Read Acts 20:1–27

HUNTER SAFETY: Never dry fire a bow (shoot it without an arrow). It could shatter and injure you or those near you.

60. GET OUT OF THE BOAT

"Then Peter got down out of the boat, walked on the water and came toward Jesus."

MATTHEW 14:29

Many black bear hunting experts believe that black bears are extremely intelligent and have a great sense of smell. Their noses are so good that some believe when they approach a bait station set up by a hunter they can smell the hunter in the tree regardless of what is done to hide human odor. The bear approaches the bait and eats simply because he is hungry and willing to take the risk of being shot. He weighs his options and knows he must eat so he digs in and hopes for the best. Sometimes he makes it to see another day; sometimes he doesn't.

FAST FACT:
The black bear is the smallest of three species of bears found in North America.

God rarely asks us to take these kinds of risks. He may ask us to step out in faith, or He might ask us to do something for Him that we aren't comfortable doing, but few of us have ever been asked by God to risk our life for Him. It is a good thing. Most of us aren't very good at taking risks.

At some point, all of us have probably felt the tug of God on our heart as He asks us to take a risk for Him. Sometimes He places something on our hearts that won't go away unless we do whatever we feel He is asking us to do. Sometimes, like the bear, we are hungry for more of what God has to offer us, but we can't seem to take the risk needed to get where we know we belong.

Several times in the Bible Christ asked His friends to take a risk. He asked Peter to step out of the boat. I'm sure Peter was never the same after that experience. Is God asking you to take a risk in your life for Him? Is He asking you to step out of the boat?

—TRACY BREEN

FOLLOW THE COMPASS

Have you ever taken a risk for God? Can you think of something He might want you to do that includes stepping out a bit?

From the Guidebook: Read Matthew 14.

HUNTING: Always spin test and shoot your hunting arrows with broadheads before you go hunting. Arrows tipped with broadheads can fly entirely different from arrows tipped with field tips, especially at great distances.

61. THE MASTER FISHERMAN

On Point:
Obeying the Master

"Simon answered, 'Master, we've worked hard all night and haven't caught anything. But because you say so, I will let down the nets.'"

LUKE 5:5

I'm a fisherman.

I know how to catch the smallmouth and walleye and panfish that inhabit the lake by our small cabin in Michigan's Upper Peninsula. I know where the fish lurk, their feeding habits, and the best times to fish. I have my own proven lures and successful strategies. So I'm reluctant to take the advice of someone who rows over and tells me how to catch the fish in "my" lake.

So I can sympathize with Peter in today's Bible reading from Luke 5. He knew how to catch fish in the Sea of Galilee. It was "his" lake, but he had been out all night and hadn't caught a thing. "Sometimes the fish just don't cooperate," I can hear him say.

Then Jesus told him, "Let down the nets for a catch" (v. 4). Peter said, "Master, we've worked hard all night and haven't caught anything. But because you say so, I will let down the nets" (v. 5). He caught so many fish, he needed help to bring them to shore! Jesus then told Peter, "From now on you will catch men" (v. 10). Jesus was more concerned that Peter learn to fish for souls.

FAST FACT:

Panfish can be any of these species: perch, crappie, white bass, candlefish, sand roller—as long as they are small enough to fit into a pan.

When it comes to fishing for souls, the issue is not how good we are at persuading people. It's whether we are obeying the Master whenever His Spirit directs us to share the gospel story. Today, "let down the nets for a catch."

—David Egner

FOLLOW THE COMPASS

Have you ever felt God nudging you to talk to someone about Jesus? What did you do? How can you better prepare for the next time that happens?

From the Guidebook: Read Luke 5:1–11.

FISHING: Sharpen your fishing hooks every time before you fish.

62. IT'S ABOUT TO GET REALLY GOOD

"He who was seated on the throne said,
'I am making everything new!' "

REVELATION 21:5

One summer I took my family salmon fishing on the Kenai River in Alaska. My 15-year-old daughter was fortunate enough to hook into a trophy king salmon. The brute turned out to be 53 inches long and tipped the scales at 65 pounds.

Our eight-hour excursion started early in the morning and we caught a few right away, but we let them all go because they were too small. Our early success was followed by a long dry spell. As the morning wore on, you could sense that hope was waning. You could tell by the looks on our faces that we were slowly losing heart. It seemed certain the day was going to end in disappointment.

FAST FACT:
The world record king salmon is 97 pounds.

If we had known that in the last hour she would catch a 65-pound wall-hanger, we would have never lost heart. We would have been waiting with great anticipation—knowing that this fishing trip was about to get really good.

Fishing trips don't usually end that way—but Christianity does.

One of the best things about the Christian faith is that Jesus tells us how the story is going to end. He hasn't filled us in on all the twists and turns, but He has told us in advance that what awaits us after this life is not more of the same—but an incredible restoration. He is going to give us the world back the way it was originally meant to be before sin and death entered the picture (Revelation 21:5). So take heart! We don't know what's going to happen, but it's going to get really good.

—JEFF OLSON

FOLLOW THE COMPASS

Commit to memory Revelation 21:4–5.

For Further Reading: To learn more about what awaits us after this life, read the short book *Epic* by John Eldredge.

FISHING OR HUNTING: Plastic sealable bags are handy for storing items under wet or raining conditions (snacks, wallet, TP, camera, etc.).

63. TRUST GOD!

"Do not worry about tomorrow, for tomorrow will worry about itself. Each day has enough trouble of its own."

MATTHEW 6:34

Many of us hunt and fish to escape the hustle and bustle of life. It's an opportunity to get away from it all and relax in the wilderness God created. Often as I wander around on a mountaintop or hike across the tundra, I realize how vast this world is; how amazing the God who created it is; and how much He cares for me and wants to take care of me.

FAST FACT:
Caribou are the only members of the deer family in which both sexes grow antlers.

This hit me when I recently went on a caribou hunt in Quebec. In Quebec, caribou rarely see people, and there are places in Quebec that have never been touched by human hands. On the last day of my hunt, I stalked within shooting distance of a large band of caribou. I noticed that they were very curious about my hunting partner, our guide, and me. They weren't afraid of us, because they hadn't ever seen humans. They are typically only afraid of what they know can hurt them—bears and wolves. Besides those animals, they don't worry about much. They continue on about their business of migrating and sleeping.

I can learn a few things from the caribou. As they wander around the countryside, God looks after each one of them, and the only time they get worked up is when danger looms.

Many of us spend countless hours of our lives worrying instead of enjoying life and realizing that God is here for us and is protecting us. The caribou worry about getting devoured by wolves and bear; that's it. We too should keep a lookout for the evil one who tries to devour us. "The thief comes only to steal and kill and destroy" (John 10:10). He uses our life circumstances to wear us down—hoping that we will lose our faith and walk away from Christ.

Staying on the lookout and realizing that the devil is alive and real is a good thing. Worrying about everything else in life isn't. Enjoy life. If God takes care of all living creatures from the birds of the air to the caribou on the tundra, surely He will take care of us.

—TRACY BREEN

FOLLOW THE COMPASS

What are you worried about today? What is the thief trying to steal from you? How can you give your worries to God and trust Him?

From the Guidebook: Read Matthew 6.

HUNTER SAFETY: Keep your finger outside the finger guard until you are ready to shoot.

64. RELAXED CHRISTIANS

*"Come with me by yourselves to a quiet place
and get some rest."*

MARK 6:31

Rest, relaxation, and recreation are essential if we are to function properly in our highly structured, tension-filled world. It's folly to think we can do our best work for the Lord with nerves taut and frayed from being constantly on the go. Jesus recognized this basic human need for diversion. When His disciples returned from a strenuous preaching mission, He didn't hustle them out and tell them to get back on the road again. Instead, He invited them to come with Him into a desert place where they could relax and be renewed.

FAST FACT:

Pigeons living in captivity can live for 15 to 20 years. Pigeon couples will mate for life, and they will raise a family of birds together.

According to tradition, when the apostle John was bishop in Ephesus, his hobby was raising pigeons. On one occasion an Ephesian elder passed his house as he returned from hunting. When he saw John playing with one of his birds, he gently chided the old bishop for spending his time so frivolously. John looked at his critic's bow and remarked that the string was loosened. "Yes," said the huntsman, "I always loosen the string of my bow when it's not in use. If it always stayed tight, it would lose its rebounding quality and fail me in the hunt." "And I," said John, "am now relaxing the bow of my mind so that I may be better able to shoot the arrows of divine truth."

While this may be only a story, it carries a pointed lesson for every child of God. He does not want us to keep the string of our lives taut at all times. Hobbies, vacations, and wholesome recreation are a part of His will for us. In fact they help us to be at our best. Unless we take time to become relaxed Christians, it won't be long until we are wrecked Christians.

—Dennis De Haan

FOLLOW THE COMPASS

It takes hard work to make a living, so it is essential to find ways to get away from life's pressures. What do you do to relax and recharge your batteries?

From the Guidebook: Read Luke 9:1–10.

HUNTING: When you scout out your deer-hunting land before the hunt begins, look for items related to the food chain. Look for trees that deer like to feed from, such as acorn-bearing trees.

65. CREATION DEFICIT DISORDER

On Point:
Listening for God's voice

"Be still, and know that I am God."
PSALM 46:10

Throughout the morning my son and I inched our way along Glacier National Park's Haystack Mountain trail. Our goal was to photograph the majesty of the Rocky Mountains and the bighorn sheep that inhabited the park. As special as the morning was, one thing puzzled me.

While we had been photographing, many hikers had passed us by. More than a few had their Walkman stereos plugged into their ears as they walked the trail, presumably to listen to their favorite music. Odd, I thought. Do they realize what they are missing?

FAST FACT:
Charles's photographic work has appeared on the covers of more than a dozen magazines.

Could the sound of the No. 1 song on the music chart be better than the sound of wind blowing through the mountains, the chatter between pine squirrels, or of the rushing water cascading over a mountain waterfall? Why would these hikers rob themselves of some of the most beautiful sounds in nature?

Sadly our plugged-in, tuned-out, over-stimulated world is being robbed of the sounds of God's creation. In the process people succumb to what I call Creation Deficit Disorder.

As you journey through today, take time to listen to God's small voices, be it the sound of rustling leaves in the wind, a blue jay squawking in the forest, or the rumbling of an approaching thunderstorm. All are God's music and far more beautiful than anything man can create.

Remember to thank Him for His symphony.

—CHARLES ALSHEIMER

FOLLOW THE COMPASS

Have you ever turned off the cell phone, walked into a nearby woods, and simply listened? Try it and discover how God can "speak" to you through the marvels of His creation. Write down the ways in which being still can help draw you toward our heavenly Father.

From the Guidebook: Read Isaiah 44:23–24.

HUNTING: In calling deer, muffle your call by putting it under a few layers of clothing. Also some calls allow you to suck in instead of blowing out, which gives a softer call. Call softer and less often.

66. ALWAYS ON TARGET

On Point:
Letting God's Word affect your life

"But his delight is in the law of the Lord, and on his law he meditates day and night."

PSALM 1:2

When a friend of mine gets ready for hunting season, he works at perfecting his archery skill with the compound bow. He sets up a target, steps back 15 yards, and shoots. When he can consistently drive all his arrows into the bull's eye, he drops back five more yards and shoots again. He does this until he hits the target with accuracy from 50 yards away. He practices and practices until his arrows strike the center of the target nearly every time.

FAST FACT:
For an amazing display of archery skills, watch this YouTube video: www.youtube. com/watch?v= j1FwNX4bC9A

The Word of God is like an archer's arrow, and it never fails to hit the intended mark. The Hebrew word for law is *torah*, which comes from a root that means, "to throw something so that it hits the mark." It refers to casting a javelin or shooting an arrow.

Teacher and author Eugene Peterson said of God's Word that it is aimed, intentional, and personal in nature. He wrote, "When we are spoken to in this way, piercingly and penetratingly, we are not the same. These words get inside us and work their meaning in us." They may give us the exact encouragement we need, or they may cut deep, exposing our motives.

When God's words strike squarely in our hearts, we should delight in them as the psalmist did (Psalm 1:2). They may hit us where it hurts, but they will meet our deepest need. They will always be on target!

—DAVID EGNER

FOLLOW THE COMPASS

What is the most convicting Bible passage you know? What is it about this passage that strikes a chord with you and challenges you?

From the Guidebook: Read Hebrews 4:11–16.

HUNTING SAFETY: Always treat a firearm as if it is loaded. When you are done, store your firearm unloaded and locked safely away.

67. A DIFFERENT POINT OF VIEW

On Point:
Developing a new perspective

"The Son of Man came to seek and to save what was lost."
LUKE 19:10

Many people have a casual view of the sport of fishing. If they have the time, they may mosey over to a nearby lake and drown a few worms. For them, it's a chance to unwind on a summer evening and reel in a fish or two.

Others take the sport more seriously. It's not something they do if they simply have the time. They *make* the time for it. These anglers plan their weekends and vacations around it. They are on the water at the crack of dawn. And they will spend hours trying to catch their limit.

FAST FACT:
Many American presidents enjoyed fishing. Among the best were Grover Cleveland, Herbert Hoover, and George H. W. Bush.

Jesus once asked a couple of fisherman to follow Him and become "fishers of men" (Matthew 4:19). This was no simple request. Catching fish was more than a sport for these commercial fishermen. It was literally a matter of life-and-death. Empty nets meant empty stomachs and empty pockets.

While there was a lot at stake for Peter and Andrew, Jesus wasn't only calling them to make a bold career move. He was also inviting them to look at their lives from a radically new perspective. Jesus was there to save lost people—which is a far cry more important than hooking fish.

Following Jesus may not require us to give up our careers, but we will never look at ourselves in the same way again if we do. As we follow Jesus, we can begin to see how and where our lives line up with His plan to find, rescue, and restore those who are lost (Luke 19:10).

The more we pursue Christ, the more we will start to understand our purpose in life from His point of view—as the One who is seeking and saving the lost.

—Jeff Olson

FOLLOW THE COMPASS

How has following Jesus and His mission changed your perspective on life?

For Further Reading: Check out the Discovery Series booklet *What Does It Take to Follow Christ?* www.discoveryseries.org/q0710.

GUN SAFETY: Never shoot a gun into the air in celebration. That bullet has to come down somewhere—and you have no control about where it might hit.

68. A STORM IS COMING!

*"Man is destined to die once, and after that
to face judgment."*

HEBREWS 9:27

We were in a small boat on the far side of the lake, and the fish were biting when we heard a rumble of thunder in the distance. Looking up, we saw a mass of dark clouds in the west.

I ignored the suggestion of my fishing partner that it might be wise to start back to the cottage—I wanted to keep fishing. Then it happened! The storm was suddenly upon us. We tried to start the motor, but it wouldn't go! My friend tried to row, but the rain came in sheets and the waves tossed our little aluminum boat. We survived, but I learned a lesson. Don't delay when a storm is brewing.

FAST FACT:

Storm tips if on a boat: Get in the middle of the boat and crouch down. Don't touch metal. Put on lifejacket. Disconnect any electrical equipment. Pray.

Another type of storm is coming—a day of judgment. It may seem far off, and you don't feel you have to hurry to prepare. You may be in good health and in the prime of life. But listen, the storm may come upon you unexpectedly.

Proverbs 1 says that disaster will strike the person who foolishly ignores all warnings (v. 27). And the author of Hebrews warned, "Just as man is destined to die once, and after that to face judgment, so Christ was sacrificed once to take away the sins of many people" (9:27).

To heed God's warnings is true wisdom. Have you sought shelter in Christ? If you haven't, it's time to stop "fishing" and seek safety before it's too late. Turn from your sin and turn to Christ. Do so today.

—MART DE HAAN

FOLLOW THE COMPASS

Do you feel that God is warning you about some part of your life? What is the next step you should take?

From the Guidebook: Read Proverbs 1:20–33.

HUNTING: Everybody loses muscle as they age—about ten pounds of muscle per decade! To decrease muscle loss and increase your ability to get around in the woods like you did when you were young, exercise regularly. Lifting weights or walking several times a week will help keep muscle loss to a minimum.

69. DISCOURAGED?

"Why are you downcast, O my soul? Why so disturbed within me? Put your hope in God, for I will yet praise him, my Savior and my God."

PSALM 42:5

When you don't own your own hunting land, it becomes increasingly difficult to find a place to hunt.

For the past few years our family has had permission to bow hunt on a farm. We have harvested some nice deer off that piece of property and have also begun to manage it for bigger bucks. Last year we saw some really nice bucks.

One spring I dropped off a gift certificate to the owner and asked if we could hunt again in the coming fall. It was then that she broke the news. She didn't have any problem with the way we had hunted, and she felt bad telling me, but things had changed in her personal situation and she would not be able to let us hunt there in the fall.

Disappointment with a capital D! We finally had places for all our family members to hunt, and each had a really good spot. Now I would have to start looking for a new piece of hunting land.

Disappointment. We all face it—in relationships, in work situations, even in our churches. Where do we turn when we are discouraged?

FAST FACT:

Maury's state, Michigan, has a Hunter Access Program that enables the state to lease private lands for use by hunters—as long as the hunters gain permission. The landowners are not liable for injuries to the hunters.

The psalmist in the Bible knew where to turn. He turned to God. He asked a key question of himself: Why am I so disquieted and disturbed within? Then he answered his own question: "Put your hope in God, for I will yet praise him, my Savior and my God."

God is the one who can come to our rescue and lift our spirits. He might even work out our situation for the better. Just watch and see!

—Maury De Young

FOLLOW THE COMPASS

Think of what things disappoint you the most. Have you really turned to God in this area?

From the Guidebook: Read Psalm 42 and 43.

HUNTING: Before embarking on your next hunting trip, check your binoculars to make sure they are still clear and that the adjustment knobs work well.

70. WHERE ARE THE FISH?

" 'Come, follow me,' Jesus said, 'and I will make you fishers of men.' "

MARK 1:17

A pastor told me a fascinating story of a church in a Canadian fishing village. The founding fathers had chosen to build the church at the rocky edge of the Atlantic Ocean. Because it was located in the center of where the fishermen and townspeople lived, the church flourished.

FAST FACT:
One beautiful example of an old Canadian fishing village is Battle Harbour in Southern Labrador.

As the congregation grew, however, the members decided to construct a new building far from the waterfront. Then an interesting thing happened. They seemed to lose their zeal for the lost after they moved. Why? Some said it was because they were no longer among the people.

We see in Mark 1 that Jesus began His ministry by walking along the Sea of Galilee and calling fishermen to be His disciples. He told them, "Follow me, and I will make you fishers of men" (v. 17).

Where are the "fish" in our communities? Do we expect them to come on their own to our church and hear the pastor present the gospel? Or have we chosen to follow Christ and become fishermen who dare to go to where the fish are, taking the message of life and hope to our schools and workplaces and neighborhoods?

Just as we won't catch fish in a kitchen sink, we can't "catch" souls if we don't go where they are.

—DAVID EGNER

FOLLOW THE COMPASS

Do you know at least five people who need the gospel of Jesus Christ? Why not make it a point to reach out to at least one of them this week with the good news?

From the Guidebook: Read Mark 1:14–20.

FISHING: If you fish in muddy water conditions, add an after-market rattle to your favorite lure. Fish use their sense of hearing more readily when they can't see in murky water.

71. WHAT ARE YOU HUNTING FOR?

"But seek first his kingdom and his righteousness, and all these things will be given to you as well."

MATTHEW 6:33

Due to media influence and peer pressure, too many of today's hunters are getting "lost" in the woods. Rather than hunting for sheer enjoyment they've turned hunting into a game where the only thing that matters is success in the field.

FAST FACT:
Among the high-tech stuff hunters use now are the following: heat sensors to find wounded animals, remote-controlled cameras, electronic duck calls, and motorized decoys.

Driven to be the best deer hunter on the planet, they put everything they have into their sport. They buy the best equipment, tirelessly practice, learn all they can about their quarry, and plan their hunts with military precision. No stone is left unturned. Their passion becomes their god. The end result is that families suffer and God becomes a footnote in the hunter's life.

Never forget that the greatest thing for the hunter is not harvesting trophy racked animals. They are what they are—things that eventually wither away and become lost in the clutter of life. The greatest things in life should be the relationship you have with your loved ones and the God who made you.

God wants us to hunt for Him on a daily basis and be passionate about Him. The God of the Bible created everything we love in the out-of-doors—and so much more. He loved us so much that He sent His son to earth to show us how to live and how to get to heaven.

When you know Jesus as your Savior and follow His teachings, you keep life in perspective. Hunting is a wonderful pastime, especially when you hunt with the Maker of the universe.

—Charles Alsheimer

FOLLOW THE COMPASS

In what ways are you hunting for God in your life? Would it help to write down three areas in which you'd like to pursue God more diligently?

From the Guidebook: Read Psalm 119:1–10.

HUNTING: After cleaning a rifle barrel, shoot it a few times before going hunting. Gun cleaning agents like oil solvents can rob a barrel of accuracy. Fouling out the barrel ahead of time will help keep the gun accurate at long distances.

72. BOUND TO BE FREE

"For he who was a slave when he was called by the Lord is the Lord's freedman."

1 CORINTHIANS 7:22

The image of a duck flying through the air with an arrow embedded in her body is still fresh in my memory. I saw the picture in a local newspaper that carried the story of a mallard duck that had eluded the attempts of rescuers to capture her and remove the foreign object. A couple of months later a Canada goose flew into Wisconsin with the same problem. A young bow hunter had hit his mark, but that didn't stop the bird. She had evaded game wardens, avoided tranquilizer-laced grain, and even dodged cannon fired nets. Finally, after about a month, the wound seemed to exhaust the goose, and she was caught with a fishing net. Surgery was performed, and it wasn't long until she was returned to freedom. If geese could think, I'm sure she'd now be wondering why in the world she had tried so hard to elude her captors for so long.

FAST FACT:
If you ever find an injured Canada goose, you can get advice for what to do at www. lovecanadageese. com/injuredgeese. html

The experience of this reluctant captive reminds me of the men Christ spoke to in John 8. They too were slow to realize the seriousness of their condition. They didn't understand the motives of the One who, to them, looked like a captor. After all, He wanted them to surrender the ultimate direction of their lives to His Spirit. He asked them to become His disciples.

He implored them to become spiritual bond-slaves. But they were unable to realize that by surrendering they could "be set free" (v. 33).

Is it possible we have forgotten that real freedom is found only in being secure in Christ? This relates not only to our ultimate salvation but also to our daily walk with the Lord. As servants of Christ, we are bound to be free.

—MART DE HAAN

FOLLOW THE COMPASS

Is there something you need to surrender to God in order to be made free? If it seems frightening to consider surrendering to God, make it a matter of prayer first.

From the Guidebook: Read John 8:31–45.

HUNTING: Use a flashlight for safety going to and returning from your stand. You can point the light down or use colored light so you won't spook the game.

73. WHAT ARE YOUR GIFTS?

On Point:
Glorifying God with your gifts

*"There are different kinds of gifts, but the same Spirit.
There are different kinds of service, but the same Lord."*

1 CORINTHIANS 12:4–5

God has gifted all of us. Some of us are gifted fishermen; some of us are gifted hunters. Others are gifted businessmen or mechanics. From time to time, I encounter people who want my job as an outdoor writer. Many of them say they don't have the gift to write or don't feel as if they are gifted at all. The grass is always greener on the other side.

I look at some of my friends who can build anything with their hands, and I wish I could be like them. Watching them build furniture, hang doors, and construct houses makes me long to be a handy person, but I am not. I am an outdoor writer and communicator. I believe that is one of the things God created me to be. Much of my writing focuses on how-to stuff: how to become a better hunter and how to hunt all over the country without breaking the bank. God has also used me to speak at outdoor game dinners and write outdoor devotions like this one. He uses my gifts to glorify himself.

You have gifts that God has given you. He wants you to use them to glorify Him. By glorifying Him with your gifts, you will feel fulfilled and discover your purpose. Deep down, most of us know what we are good at. The problem is that we often hide our gifts or think somebody else's gifts are better than ours. The Bible says if we use our gifts to glorify God, God will grant us more gifts (Matthew 25:29). Go on. Use the talents God has blessed you with. What are you afraid of? Receiving more gifts from God?

—TRACY BREEN

FOLLOW THE COMPASS

How has God used you and your gifts to glorify Him? Take a spiritual gifts test to help you determine your gifts: www.churchgrowth.org/cgi-cg/gifts.cgi?intro=1

From the Guidebook: Read Matthew 25:14–30.

HUNTING: If you hunt over mock scrapes, make sure you build a licking branch. Deer often lick and rub a licking branch to let other deer know who has visited the scrape. The majority of scrapes built by deer have a licking branch overhead. A mock scrape appears more authentic if it has a licking branch.

74. SUNDAY HYPOCRITES

On Point:
Living every day for Jesus

"On the outside you appear to people as righteous, but on the inside you are full of hypocrisy and wickedness."

MATTHEW 23:28

I read about a man known as "Grandpa Hicks," who made his living by crooked means. He trapped fish illegally in a lake near his home. He rented out boats that didn't belong to him and pocketed the money. He stole gasoline for his motorboat from boats at a neighboring dock. And he would steal catfish from the lines of other fishermen. He seemed to have no conscience about such matters.

One Sunday morning two of his grandchildren asked if he'd take them fishing. With great conviction he replied, "I never fish on Sundays. I wasn't brought up like that!"

This man reminds me of the Pharisees Jesus talked about in Matthew 23. He branded them as those who deprived widows of their homes (v. 14); those who lacked justice, mercy, and faith (v. 23); and those who were greedy (v. 25). Yet they were the very ones who wanted to kill Jesus for healing on the Sabbath (Matthew 12:9–14). Both Grandpa Hicks and the Pharisees placed greater value on the legalistic observance of a day than on a holy life.

Every believer should benefit from fellowship, worship, and instruction on the Lord's Day. But if Sunday observance

FAST FACT:

In colonial America, some areas had blue laws that outlawed things like fishing and other recreation on Sunday. In New York in 1700, the punishment for such an offense was three hours in stocks.

serves as a coverup for the way we live the other six days of the week, then like Grandpa Hicks, we are Sunday hypocrites.

—RICHARD DE HAAN

FOLLOW THE COMPASS

Should there be any difference in the way you treat others and live for Jesus between Sunday and the other days of the week?

From the Guidebook: Read Matthew 23:23–28.

FISHING: Shredded paper works well for worm bedding and is not as messy.

75. WHEN DOUBTS ARISE— LOOK UP!

"Restore to me the joy of your salvation."
PSALM 51:12

Sometimes Christians confuse a temporary loss of the joy of their salvation with a loss of their salvation itself. Because of unconfessed sin, broken fellowship with God, or a decrease in their love for their fellow believers, they do not feel the underlying joy in Christ they once knew. Because the feeling is gone, they conclude that their salvation is gone as well. But how wrong they are!

The following experience will help to illustrate this problem: I was sitting in my rowboat on Piatt Lake about midnight, fishing for pike. The air was calm, and the surface of the lake was like glass. The moon, full and silvery, was reflected perfectly in the still water, and I marveled at the awesome sight. Then I whimsically cast a lure into the reflection, and it looked as if the moon had been shattered into a thousand pieces. Now, I would have been foolish to think that some lunar explosion had suddenly shattered the moon itself. All I had to do was look up into the sky to reassure myself that the moon was still there—shining brightly and unchanged.

When David prayed for forgiveness after his terrible sins of adultery and murder, he asked the Lord to restore the "joy" of

FAST FACT:
At night, sometimes pike respond best when they hear a sound above them—as if something had dropped into the water. This stirs them up a bit.

his salvation—not salvation itself. May we too realize that losing the feeling of being saved is like shattering the reflection of the moon. Just as the moon remains unchanged, so our salvation is still secure. When doubts arise, look up! Assurance will return.

—DAVID EGNER

FOLLOW THE COMPASS

Do you doubt sometimes? What helps? Does it help to spend time raising your voice and your attention to God—"looking up" as the article suggests?

From the Guidebook: Read Psalm 51:1–13.

FISHING: When fishing for pike, you may notice that a pike will hit the bait and let go a few times. Pike have a big appetite, so be patient. He'll be back.

76. ELK CARE

"Does he not leave the ninety-nine in the open country and go after the lost sheep until he finds it?"

LUKE 15:4

Next to deer, elk are one of the most sought-after big game animals in North America. People enjoy hunting them so much because the bulls bugle to each other and to the cows. The screaming bugle at daylight is one of those noises that makes the hair on the back of your neck stand up.

Although the bugle sounds impressive, one of the things that impresses me most about a bull elk is the way he cares for his cows. A typical bull has between five and twenty-five cows in his harem. As the females feed in a meadow, the bull typically feeds with them. When he decides it's time to mosey on to another place, he herds up his ladies like a cowboy herding cattle. If he thinks one is getting too far away, he runs out and hits her in the rear end with his antlers to get her to move in the right direction.

FAST FACT:

There are four living subspecies of elk in North America.

Seeing this always reminds me of how Christ takes care of us. He leaves the flock to find the one that strayed. Sometimes we need a kick in the pants to wake us up and help us realize we have strayed from where we belong. Sometimes it takes a painful experience to wake us up. Other times, a gentle push is required. In both cases, God loves us and keeps track of us. He pulls us in when He sees fit, even if it takes a push in the right direction that might hurt a little.

—TRACY BREEN

FOLLOW THE COMPASS

Has God ever had to go out of His way to pull you close to Him? What did it teach you about God's love for you?

From the Guidebook: Read Luke 15.

HUNTING: Are you thinking about planting a food plot to hunt over? Think small. Small food plots offer better bowhunting opportunities, cost less to plant, and are easier to maintain than large fields.

77. LIMITED EDITION

On Point:
Honoring God's handiwork

"For we are God's workmanship, created in Christ Jesus to do good works."

EPHESIANS 2:10

The turkey turned my way. I decided to stop calling and wait him out. As he got closer, I could see that he had a nice beard. His head turned from white to red and then back to white again.

This tom turkey must have gotten too close to the neighborhood of a red-winged blackbird, because that bird started dive bombing and pecking at the turkey's head. At every encounter the turkey would duck down and run a few feet. I could easily adjust and get into position.

The turkey kept coming, but he seemed to be getting more nervous. I decided he was close enough and gently pulled the trigger; he went down right there.

As I approached the bird, I was amazed at this magnificent creature! The sun was just starting to settle in the west, and its light reflected off his feathers. What an incredible sight! I fell on my knees and thanked God for this awesome gift. As I looked at the bird again, I knew that even the best artist could not match the beauty of what I saw.

When it comes to our lives, we often find beauty and self-worth in what we accom-

FAST FACT:

The National Wild Turkey Federation works hard to increase the population of turkeys and preserve their natural habitat. It is estimated that there are more than 6 million wild turkeys in the US. In the 1930s, there were only about 30,000 birds.

plish. However, that's a pretty shaky standard. God gives us a better standard. He says we are his limited edition (1 of 1). We are his work of art. He is the one designing our lives. He is right on schedule. He doesn't make any mistakes. And he has never gotten a B, C, D, E, or F grade in art.

—MAURY DE YOUNG

FOLLOW THE COMPASS

Talk to someone who has just retired, who has had to take a medical leave, or just lost his job. Notice how easy it is for someone to base his identity and worth on what we do. Will you trust God's perspective of your life and find your security in Him instead of your own performance?

From the Guidebook: Read Psalm 139:13–17.

HIKING: When hiking for long distances always wear two pairs of socks: one thin pair next to the skin and a thicker outer pair. The thin pair will keep moisture away from your feet while the outer pair cushions your feet and prevents hotspots and blisters from forming.

78. THE ULTIMATE GUIDE

"Jesus answered, 'I am the way and the truth and the life. No one comes to the Father except through me.' "

JOHN 14:6

Many hunters dream of taking a once-in-a-lifetime hunt. Because of the high cost of a special hunt, it is important for the hunter to know the game he will be pursuing, the best time to hunt, and the best way to get to the hunting location. Such hunts also require hiring a reputable outfitter for any hope of success.

FAST FACT:

Looking for elk, cougars, or mule deer? It could cost you $4,000 for a several-day hunt with a good outfitter.

A good outfitter is one who has good accommodations and people skills, knows the country, the animals that will be hunted, and how to put the hunter in a position to harvest an animal.

If you've never hunted with a particular outfitter, you know that a lot of faith is required in the booking process. Unfortunately, too often hunts don't work out as planned. Poor connections and accommodations or an absence of game are a few of the reasons dream hunts turn into bad dreams.

I've taken many outfitted hunts in my career and sad to say some were real nightmares, which taught me a thing or two along the way. One thing I've learned is that if you put your faith in man there is a good chance he will eventually let you down.

I've also learned this. If you want to travel life's road with the best outfitter in the business, you need to book life's dream hunt with Jesus Christ because He truly is the way, the truth, and the life. He will never lead you astray, He will always take care of you, and He will show you how to find eternal life.

—CHARLES ALSHEIMER

FOLLOW THE COMPASS

Have you ever heard people criticize Christianity because it is "too narrow"? But if God is truly the creator, does He not have the right to set the guidelines for who gets into His heaven? And if Jesus is not the only way, was His death not then a wasted excursion to earth? Spend time investigating Jesus' claim as the "way and the truth and the life."

From the Guidebook: Read John 14:1–6.

HUNTING: Shoot a few arrows or fire a few rounds through your gun after a road trip. Airlines and truck beds can be tough on hunting equipment. Discovering that your sights are off in the field can ruin a good day of hunting and a rare opportunity to fill the freezer with organic meat.

79. ARE YOU ON THE RIGHT PATH?

On Point:
Trusting God for your future

"Be strong and courageous. Do not be afraid or terrified because of them, for the Lord your God goes with you; he will never leave you nor forsake you."

DEUTERONOMY 31:6

I have always been fascinated by the nose of a good bird dog.

When my wife and I first got married, I had a German shorthaired pointer and a German wirehaired pointer. Both dogs had their strengths and weaknesses, but both dogs had great noses. I remember hunting ducks in a marsh with my wirehair. It was a dry year, and there wasn't much water in the marsh. After shooting a mallard and watching the pile of cattails the bird fell into, I told my dogs to fetch it up. After a long search and no bird, I went over to help her find the duck. As I approached the area where I thought the duck was, my dog headed in a different direction. I wondered where she was going. Moments later, she dove headfirst into the mud under a log and appeared with the duck. She relied on her sense of smell and knew exactly where to go. Over time, she learned to trust her senses, knowing that they never let her down.

FAST FACT:
The human nose has roughly 5 million scent receptors. A dog's nose has over 200 million scent receptors. No wonder dogs are so great at finding ducks.

Has your faith ever led you down a path you weren't sure about, but you sensed it was where God was leading you? As with my dog, when you dive into the mud, things can get messy. Sometimes people think you are crazy or try to pull you in a different direction as I almost did with my dog. However, having faith and relying on God when we are not sure where we are going is what God wants us to do. His Word says to trust Him, and He won't leave us or forsake us. He will see us through until the end.

—TRACY BREEN

FOLLOW THE COMPASS

Has there ever been a path in life you weren't sure you wanted to go down—but you felt God was leading you there? What has that experience taught you?

From the Guidebook: Read Acts 2:28

HUNTING: Have you had a bad experience with deer urine while hunting? Deer urine often breaks down while sitting on the store shelf, and then it spooks deer. To ensure that you are getting fresh urine, purchase deer lure that has a batch date on the bottle. Better yet, buy urine that is frozen the day it is collected and sold frozen in the bottle.

80. THE LESSON OF THE OSPREY

On Point:
Marveling at God's creation

"I gave him the wasteland as his home,
the salt flats as his habitat."

JOB 39:6

On a beautiful late summer evening, my friend Steve and I were fishing lazily from our little boat on Piatt Lake, hoping a splashing pike or swirling bass would strike at our lures. An osprey circled quietly overhead. We watched him with detached interest realizing vaguely that he was doing the same thing we were doing—fishing. He was hovering over one area when suddenly he went into a power dive, shattering the stillness as he crashed feet first into the water. Then he arose majestically, holding a large fish by his sharp talons.

FAST FACT:
The osprey ranges worldwide, and it is relatively the same wherever it is found.

Later, I did a little research and discovered that these fish hawks, as they are commonly called, are 22 to 25 inches long and have a 5- to 6-foot wingspan. They live near water, returning to the same nest year after year by driving off all competitors and reserving their lake or section of ocean for themselves. Their long, pointed wings give them both the power to dive and the control to hover. Keen eyesight lets them see several feet below the water's surface. And their claws are perfectly designed to help them hold firmly the fish they grab. What a marvel of creation! God made the osprey perfect for his environment.

God's questions to Job in today's Scripture were intended to cause him to see His marvelous design and power in His creatures, and arouse in him a sense of awe and wonder. Does our observation of God's creatures do the same for us?

—DAVID EGNER

FOLLOW THE COMPASS

What are your favorite expressions of God's creation? What does each teach you about God's amazing creative ability?

From the Guidebook: Read Job 39:19–30.

HUNTING: A strap-on step is easy to assemble and adjust. It works well for hanging items such as a backpack, binoculars, or even your bow.

81. SERIOUS ABOUT FISHING

On Point:
Fulfilling God's commands

"[Jesus] saw two brothers, Simon called Peter and his brother Andrew. They were casting a net into the lake, for they were fishermen."

MATTHEW 4:18

I'm amused by the story of the boy who was fishing in a stream when a group of teenagers arrived on the scene with their rods and reels and fancy flies. They thrashed the water as they joked and laughed, casting and reeling in repeatedly but catching nothing.

The boy sat intently watching the tip of his tree-branch pole. Every so often he pulled up a fish. Finally one of the fellows shouted, "How do you do it? We've got special flies, but we're not catching anything!" The boy looked up long enough to reply, "I'm fishing for fish. You're fishing for fun."

FAST FACT:

Comedian Stephen Wright observed, "There's a fine line between fishing and standing on the shore like an idiot."

At least four of Christ's disciples were fishermen. They knew that it took their full attention and energies to catch fish. Therefore, when Christ commanded them to leave their nets and "catch men," they realized it would demand their all.

That's how we should view our part in fulfilling the Great Commission (Matthew 28:16–20). Making Christ known is not an optional pastime for the excitement it may bring or the stories we can tell of souls won. It is serious business, requiring prayer, courage, sacrifice, perseverance, and singleminded purpose.

We should all be fishing for lost people. We can give out tracts, invite friends to church, and tell others about Christ. Are we serious about it?

—Paul Van Gorder

GET SERIOUS

What are you the most serious about in life? Does it have anything to do with influencing others to trust Jesus? What is something you can do to increase your interest in doing that?

Go Deep: Read Matthew 4:18–22.

HUNTING: Use an occasional soft doe grunt as you are walking through the woods and you will be surprised how close you can get to deer.

82. CAMPING FOR PRAISE

*"Praise him, sun and moon, praise him,
all you shining stars."*

PSALM 148:3

Are you a camper? If so, you understand the greatness of being in a spot where you can look up into the night and see God's grandeur. Away from the city lights, you can more readily see the night sky as God designed it.

To me, the spacious nighttime canopy of stars that covers an outdoor panorama of twinkling stars is among the greatest sights on earth. Sure, the Grand Canyon is awe-inspiring, and the Rocky Mountains are nothing if not spectacular. Green forests are majestic in their stillness, and the ocean's power cannot be described.

FAST FACT:
*More than
50 million
Americans go
tent camping
each year.*

But peering into the night sky creates in my mind thoughts of God's greatness that surpass what can be found on earth. That view into the deep recesses of space allows me to wonder at the unfathomable power of God's creative ability. It makes me look into the face of stars that are millions and millions of miles away, separated from my planet by light-years of space that God, in His mysterious perfection, inserted at creation. My mind is boggled and blessed at the same time as I stand amazed by God's creativity and His handiwork (and as I stand there, I also wonder again why He bothered making mosquitoes).

I wonder if the psalmist sometimes camped out under the stars, unobstructed as they were by the lights that dim them before our vision. I wonder if he looked into the vast array of night-lights and said, "Praise the Lord from the heavens, praise him in the heights above" (Psalm 148:1).

The praise found in Psalm 148 is the kind of God-directed thinking I can understand as I stand under a summer's night sky, chilled with the reality of what God has done for us through the miracle of creation.

—DAVE BRANON

FOLLOW THE COMPASS

God's creation gives us so much to contemplate—so much to praise Him for. List what you consider the five most awesome things God has created. Then thank Him for His workmanship.

From the Guidebook: Read Psalm 148.

FISHING WITH KIDS: Value the experience more than "catching." Catching will come later.

83. CASTING LESSONS

"Let your conversation be always full of grace, seasoned with salt, so that you may know how to answer everyone."

COLOSSIANS 4:6

A friend of mine, an avid fly fisherman, showed me pictures of some of his greatest catches—including a 170-pound tarpon he landed while on a fishing excursion in Costa Rica.

I've always enjoyed the sport as well, and our conversation prompted me to go home and reminisce on my own experiences. As I thumbed through photo albums, I found pictures of myself fly fishing in some of the most scenic rivers in the world—including places such as New Zealand, Montana, and Wyoming. Yet I noticed that I don't have a single picture of me with a fish. That's because, despite all my attempts, I haven't caught one yet.

FAST FACT:
Want to know more about fly-fishing? Go to www.flyfishing. com.

One of the major reasons so many anglers, including myself, fail is that they neglect to approach properly the fish they're trying to catch. They improperly cast the fly, and as a result they cause the fish to sense that they're being attacked instead of being offered something to eat.

This same principle can be applied to how we as Christians present the gospel to non-believers. If we cause people we're sharing Christ with to feel attacked, they are going to flee. That is why 2 Timothy 4:2 tells us to, "Preach the Word; be prepared in season and out of season; correct, rebuke and encourage—

with great patience and careful instruction." Colossians 4:6 adds, "Let your conversation be always full of grace, seasoned with salt, so that you may know how to answer everyone."

Ultimately, the most important thing we can do as we follow Christ is to become fishers of men. But first, we need to know how to cast.

—ROXANNE ROBBINS

FOLLOW THE COMPASS

Write a note of thanks to a person who has helped draw you closer to the Lord through his or her words and example.

From the Guidebook: Read Matthew 4:18–21.

FISHING: If you are wearing waders for fly fishing, always wear a wading belt to keep water out of your waders.

84. LITTLE NICKS— BIG TROUBLE!

On Point:
Getting rid of "little" sins

"A little yeast works through the whole batch of dough."

GALATIANS 5:9

We couldn't figure it out. My son and I had purchased an old powerboat for fishing and couldn't make it run properly. We were unable to get it up to speed, and it shuddered when we tried to go faster. We figured that the trouble was with the fuel system, so we adjusted the carburetor and changed the fuel filter. But that still didn't solve the problem.

When we took the boat out of the water, my son found the cause of the trouble. One of the propeller fins had a 3/4-inch (2 cm) nick in it. That can't be it, I thought. That nick is too small. But when we installed a new propeller, what a difference it made! We had been slowed down by a tiny nick.

A similar problem is often at work in our lives as Christians. Sinful practices like those described in Galatians 5:16–21 have their roots in the seemingly insignificant thoughts and attitudes of the heart (Matthew 5:28; 15:18–19). If we ignore or tolerate these "little" sins, they will eventually grow, corrupting more of our thoughts and actions—even harming people around us. Just as a little yeast "works through" a whole lump of dough (Galatians 5:9), so also a "little"

FAST FACT:
It is recommended that if you have a propeller-driven boat you keep a spare propeller in the boat—just in case.

sin can eventually weaken our service for Christ and the ministry of His church.

Remember, little nicks can cause big trouble.

—DAVID EGNER

FOLLOW THE COMPASS

What are a couple of "small" sins that you have tried to keep secret from everyone? Wouldn't it be better to ask forgiveness and get them off your back?

From the Guidebook: Read Galatians 5:16–26.

HUNTING: Do you want to see more wildlife on your property? Just add water. Biologists say that adding a watering hole to a piece of property will increase the number of deer, turkey, and other game animals that frequent the property. Dig a small depression or place half of a plastic drum in the woods and let rainwater fill it.

85. GET RECHARGED

"I am the vine; you are the branches. If a man remains in me and I in him, he will bear much fruit; apart from me you can do nothing."

JOHN 15:5

Those of us who enjoy fishing know that batteries need to be recharged. We are not as much aware of that with our vehicles that have alternators, but trolling motors need frequent recharging.

Our family often goes up to "the cottage" on weekends. At least some of us do some fishing over the weekend and usually use the trolling motor quite a bit. If we stay for a few days, it is no problem as we can plug in the trolling motor at night and be ready for the next day. However, if we fish the last day, I don't like to leave the charge on all week while we are gone. It is an automatic charger, but I don't like having a cord running out to the water with neighborhood kids playing around the area. So if we fished the last day, and someone wants to fish right away when they get there the next week, they might find a nearly dead battery.

FAST FACT:

Bass Tournament boats have either a 24-volt system (two batteries) or a 36-volt system (three batteries) that need to be recharged—plus one other starting battery for the outboard.

In life we are often like that battery; we run out of energy. On a normal, routine day we may not notice, but if we face some challenge in life, we suddenly find we don't have enough energy to handle it.

Jesus tells us that He is the source of energy. He says, "Remain in me." He goes on to say, "apart from me you can do nothing."

Jesus says that if we stay connected to Him, we will bear much fruit. Love, joy, peace, patience, self-control, and other good qualities will naturally flow from our lives if we are hooked up to the power source: Jesus.

—MAURY DE YOUNG

FOLLOW THE COMPASS

Are you plugged in? Do you have a good connection?

Do you need a recharge? Has your spiritual tank run dry? How much evidence is there of the good fruit in your life?

From the Guidebook: Read Galatians 5:22.

HUNTING: Everyone enjoys hanging his or her trophy of a lifetime over the fireplace, but according to taxidermists, the heat from a fire dries out a mount in a hurry and causes the hide to crack and look old quickly. To keep your trophy looking good, hang it on a wall that is away from a fireplace and out of direct sunlight.

86: DEAD GIVEAWAY

"By your words you will be acquitted, and by your words you will be condemned."

MATTHEW 12:37

She had never been fishing before, but to spend time with Willie, Lucy told him she loved to fish. He was happy to find a woman who could share his obsession with fishing tackle, drop-offs, and water temperature.

When they got to Willie's favorite fishing spot, the fish weren't biting but Lucy didn't care. The sun was shining and the water lapped gently at the sides of the boat. To be with Willie was all that mattered. After an hour of sharing his fishing patience, Lucy said, "Willie, you know that red and white thing you put on my line?" "You mean the bobber?" he replied. "Yeah, how much did it cost?" "Oh, about 50 cents." "Well," Lucy said, "then I owe you 50 cents because mine just sank." The truth was out. Lucy's words revealed that she actually knew very little about fishing.

Sooner or later our words unmask the true condition of our heart. Hearts filled with love for God are known by words of honesty, gratefulness, love, encouragement, wise counsel, and concern for others. Hearts filled with self-centeredness are revealed by deceit, criticism, complaining, broken confidences, and insults. Jesus said that by our words we will be judged (Matthew 12:37).

FAST FACT:

If you want to fish over one area and keep your hook at a certain level, use either a pencil-style bobber or a round bobber. And be patient.

Father, let our words today reflect our love for You, and show that Christ is living in us.

—Mart De Haan

FOLLOW THE COMPASS

If someone were to characterize the words you most commonly use, what would that person say? Would the words point people toward or away from God.

From the Guidebook: Read Matthew 12:33–37.

HUNTING: Wet wipes work well in removing camo from your face.

87. SPEND WISELY

"Do not store up for yourselves treasures on earth, where moth and rust destroy, and where thieves break in and steal. But store up for yourselves treasures in heaven."

MATTHEW 6:19–20

Most serious hunters—especially bowhunters—spend a lot of time preparing for deer season. Bowhunters are known for being a little obsessive when it comes to testing their equipment. Most bowhunters shoot their bows for hours daily all summer in preparation for the fall hunting season. In addition to shooting their bows, most bowhunters scout hunting areas, hang tree stands, plant food plots, and check scouting cameras for evidence that a big buck is lurking near their hunting area.

FAST FACT:
Hunters and anglers spend roughly $70 billion a year on hunting and fishing in America.

Bowhunters (and hunters in general) do all of this preseason preparation to increase their odds of bagging a buck. Most seasoned hunters know that the opportunity to score on a buck is often few and far between, so they do everything in their power to make the few chances they get each season count. Why do we care so much about shooting a buck? In most cases it boils down to bragging rights. We love showing off the rack to our buddies and proving that we are great hunters. To many hunters, a large-racked buck is treasured more than most things they own. I have seen many men give up everything they have for the chance to shoot a large buck.

Imagine what kind of Bible scholars we could be if we spent half of the time we spend drooling over big bucks reading the Bible! We would be more knowledgeable about the Bible, better parents, spouses, and friends to those around us. Instead of accumulating large-racked bucks, we would accumulate treasure in heaven. What are you storing up?

—Tracy Breen

FOLLOW THE COMPASS

How much time do you spend reading the Bible and other related material? How does your outlook on life change after reading God's Word?

From the Guidebook: Read Matthew 6.

HUNTING: Make sure your tree stand isn't covered with black ice before you step on it.

88. THE ULTIMATE HUNT

"For since the creation of the world God's invisible qualities—his eternal power and divine nature—have been clearly seen, being understood from what has been made, so that men are without excuse."

ROMANS 1:20

My father introduced me to deer hunting when I was five years old. It was an exciting time for me. Our time together helped us bond as a father and son, and the lessons he taught me helped lay the foundation for an incredible life. My early encounters with New York's whitetails not only taught me a lot about the natural world but they also helped introduce me to God.

Because I was an inquisitive youngster, my early forays into the woods, whether to hunt deer or pick blackberries, kept me coming back to the same question. Who made this? As I grew into manhood, the awesomeness of the natural world kept me hunting for nature's creator.

FAST FACT:
Go to the Web site www.christian bowhunters.org to find a copy of Charles's life story and testimony.

They say if you hunt hard enough you'll eventually catch up to what you are looking for. My hunt for God intensified, and in the spring of 1971, just as spring's wildflowers were beginning to bloom, I was introduced to Jesus Christ by a friend. My hunt was over.

As I reflect on my past I'm in awe of what God has done in my life. He's given me an incredible family, an exciting career, and a great country to live in. But most of all He has given me eternal life through His son Jesus.

Hunting white-tailed deer is the greatest hunting experience for many. But as exciting as it can be, it isn't the ultimate hunt. The ultimate hunt takes place when you seek and find the Maker of the white-tailed deer. That's when you bag the biggest prize, the gift of eternity offered by Jesus Christ.

—CHARLES ALSHEIMER

FOLLOW THE COMPASS

What is your story of faith? Have you ever tried to write it out to share with others? Perhaps this could be a way to reach out to unsaved friends.

From the Guidebook: Read Galatians 4:6-7.

HUNTING: Deer and other game animals can see the ultraviolet rays given off by garments that are produced with brighteners that make hunting clothes appear bright and clean on store shelves. These ultraviolet rays make hunters stand out in the woods. To eliminate the UV glow, spray your hunting clothes with an ultraviolet killer spray.

89. THE BUZZING OF THE FLIES

"If my people would but listen to me."
PSALM 81:13

I was listening to the guys at a fishing resort in Canada. "Worst year for flies we've ever seen!" "Man, you need a shotgun to protect yourself, they're so huge." "No bug spray works this year."

The bite of the black fly creates wounds that swell, get red, and itch like crazy. Get several and life is miserable—even when the fish are biting.

FAST FACT:
Although black flies are hard to stop—even with repellents—one thing that might help is that they seem to be attracted to dark clothing more than light-colored clothing.

That is nothing compared with what happened when the fourth plague hit Egypt (Exodus 8:20–24). As Moses predicted, the air was thick with swarms of flies. They invaded Pharaoh's palace, filled the houses of the officials, and were found everywhere in Egypt—except in the land of Goshen where the Israelites lived.

By this time Pharaoh should have been listening intently to every word Moses said. But after the flies were gone he hardened his heart (v. 32), and so he set himself and his people up for even more serious judgments from the Lord.

Sometimes the Lord uses drastic measures to get our attention. The "swarms of flies" take different forms—trouble, recurring failure, guilt, the hurt looks of the people we love. Those are the times we especially need to listen to God.

So let's listen carefully to the Lord while it is still quiet—before the buzzing of the flies begins.

—DAVID EGNER

FOLLOW THE COMPASS

When is the best time for you to "listen" to the Lord? When does He best communicate with you? Begin to maximize your time with Him by setting that time aside.

From the Guidebook: Read Exodus 8:20–32.

HUNTING: Animals can be repelled by human odor. Studies show that one third of all human odors are given off from the neck up. To reduce human odor, brush your teeth, take a shower, and wear an activated carbon mask when hunting. Some odor eliminating gum and lozenges are also available. It doesn't take much effort to eliminate a large portion of human odor.

90. JAWBONE CREDIT

On Point:
Keeping your vows

*"Simply let your 'Yes' be 'Yes,' and your 'No,' 'No';
anything beyond this comes from the evil one."*

MATTHEW 5:37

In 1878, a merchant in Bozeman, Montana, extended to Andrew Garcia what was called "jawbone credit." Without putting anything into writing, he gave Garcia $300 worth of supplies for a hunting and trapping expedition. The trapper promised to return and pay his debt with hides and pelts from his expedition.

FAST FACT:

Bozeman, Montana, was named for a man from Georgia who went West looking for gold and established a trail that went through the area that is now Bozeman.

While Garcia was away, hostile Indians moved into the area around Bozeman. Weather conditions got bad. Fellow trappers told him to forget about returning to Bozeman, but Garcia wouldn't hear of it. After a series of harrowing experiences, he returned to the merchant with hides and pelts to pay his debt. He kept his word.

It seems that we can't put that much stock in verbal promises these days. Many people make pledges but fail to keep them. Every divorce means at least one person has broken a sacred vow. People in trouble with the law may promise to change their ways if only they can have another chance. But when they receive clemency, they often forget the vows they had made.

God too makes vows, but He always keeps His word. If He didn't, we would have no basis for hope. Let's thank Him for being a God of integrity, and then we should resolve that we will be people whose word can be trusted.

—HERB VANDER LUGT

FOLLOW THE COMPASS

Are there any vows that you are struggling to keep? How can the words of this article help encourage you to keep them?

From the Guidebook: Read Matthew 5:33–37.

HUNTING: If you are using decoys while hunting geese, the more decoys, the better. It gives the geese a sense of security.

91. HE CALLS ME FRIEND

"I have called you friends."
JOHN 15:15

A man I know recently went big lake fishing on a charter boat out of the port of Grand Haven, Michigan. He and his friends had an incredible trip. The salmon were big (many of them were well over 15 pounds), and they were biting. By the time their 7-hour trip was over, they had hooked into 19 fish and managed to land 11.

FAST FACT:

As many as 4 million salmon are stocked into Lake Michigan in a year.

Before they ever dropped a line in the water that morning, though, the captain took the time to explain how the program was going to work. From downriggers to dispy-divers, he showed them how they set the lines and what to do when a fish strikes. Rather than treat them like spectators, he considered them to be a vital part of his crew. He treated them like valuable deck hands and invited them to get in on as much of the action as possible. He believed the more they felt like one of the crew, the more involved they would get.

The captain's approach reminds me of how Jesus thinks about His followers. Speaking to some of His first disciples, Jesus said, "I no longer call you servants, because a servant does not know his master's business. Instead, I have called you friends, for everything that I learned from my Father I have made known to you" (John 15:15).

Jesus does not mean for us to feel left out and watch His kingdom advance from a distance. He invites us to join Him as His friends and allies in the business at hand of attempting great things for Him and for others.

—JEFF OLSON

FOLLOW THE COMPASS

How would you describe your relationship with God? As a friend, or as something else? Why?

From the Guidebook: Read James 2:23

HUNTER SAFETY: Always point the muzzle in a safe direction.

92. A TRUSTY BRITTANY

*"Trust in the Lord with all your heart and lean
not on your own understanding."*

PROVERBS 3:5

I was hunting over my Brittany in a tall grass field that had often produced good results. This afternoon was different. I didn't have one point in the entire field.

FAST FACT:

The American Kennel Club lists 26 different breeds of sporting dogs divided among pointers, retrievers, setters, and spaniels.

I called my dog and headed down to work the area near a stream, thinking that the heat had moved the birds closer to water.

Walking along I suddenly realized my dog was not with me. Finally I saw him. He had drifted back to a brushy corner we had already covered and was locked on point. I moved over and got in position for a shot. At that point two quail flushed, and I was able to get a double. It was good that I had trusted my dog and not called him off.

The Bible talks about trust. It tells us to trust in the Lord with all our heart, and not to lean on our own understanding.

In the field I have learned to follow my dog. I pay attention to the wind and consider which way is best for working a field, but I have learned to trust his ability to scent birds.

In life, we often do the opposite. We trust ourselves, our own judgment, our own way of doing things. God's way is different. What He expects us to accomplish requires trusting

Him completely and not just figuring life out ourselves. Are you ready to trust?

—MAURY DE YOUNG

FOLLOW THE COMPASS

Look at your life. In what areas are you leaning more upon yourself and your experience and training instead of relying more on God? Will you trust Him completely?

From the Guidebook: Read Psalm 20:7–8 and Romans 10:11.

HUNTING: Small game hunting with a bow and arrow can be fun and challenging. With a few arrows and a couple of judo points, you can have fun for hours and practice on your yardage estimation so when you have a shot at a big buck, you will hit where you're aiming instead of shooting over his back.

93. DON'T HOLD BACK

"For whoever wants to save his life will lose it, but whoever loses his life for me and for the gospel will save it. What good is it for a man to gain the whole world, yet forfeit his soul?"

MARK 8:35–36

My father is a full-time taxidermist. Growing up, I noticed that almost every customer had two things in common. They loved to discuss hunting, and they loved to show off their trophies. After all, that was why they were at a taxidermist in the first place—to get another trophy for the wall. This allowed them to tell all of their buddies about the exciting hunt they had. Some hunters carry around photos of animals they killed—like many of us carry photos of our families.

FAST FACT:
The "father of modern taxidermy" is John Hancock, an English ornithologist, who worked his craft in the mid-1850s.

Many of my dad's customers are Christian men. Although they are eager to share hunting stories, they are not very eager to share their faith. The thought of being rejected by someone you share the gospel with is often what stops most of us from spreading the word of Christ. What if someone laughs at us? What if someone looks at us like we are crazy? What if I lose a friendship by sharing the gospel?

God wants us to be more eager about sharing our faith than we are to wear camouflage clothes and tell hunting stories. There is a variety of ways that you can share your faith without shoving the gospel down someone's throat. Outdoor tracts written by famous outdoorsmen and outdoor devotionals like this one you are reading can be distributed at the sports shop, at work, and to strangers you see wearing camouflage. Don't hold back. Find a way to spread the gospel of Christ.

—Tracy Breen

FOLLOW THE COMPASS

Write down the names of three unsaved friends you would like to give an outdoor tract or devotional to. Make sure you pray for those individuals daily and when the Lord leads you, give them the outdoorsman literature.

From the Guidebook: Read Mark 8.

HUNTING: To help you distinguish between a button buck and a doe, look at the head. An older doe will have a much longer head.

94. TAKE TIME

*"Within your temple, O God, we meditate
on your unfailing love."*

PSALM 48:9

A friend and I were on our way to the hardware store when we decided to make a quick stop for donuts in a small coffee shop. As we were talking, my friend stopped and pointed to a poster tacked on the wall behind the counter. It showed a peaceful lake scene. A father and son were visible through the early morning mist, fishing in a rowboat. All was quiet and serene. The boat was not moving on the still water, and the fishermen were watching two motionless bobbers on the placid lake. The silence and stillness left an overwhelming impression. In the corner of the poster were printed these two words: Take time.

FAST FACT:

"Getting a hobby" is in the Top 10 tips for relieving stress, and one of the best stress-reducing hobbies is fishing.

Those two words sound like a foreign language to us. We tend to speed along in life much like we drive our cars on the freeways—going faster than we should. Our lives are a blur of frantic activity. We're in the "fast lane," traveling as quickly as our bodies and minds will allow. In so doing, we often forget about God.

Yes, even though the busyness of our lives is made up of worthwhile activities, including our work and service in the church, we may have left Him back in the dust somewhere. We need to slow down and do as the writer of Psalm 48 did. He thought about God and His lovingkindness. And that takes time.

If you don't think you have time to pause from the race of life once in a while, think again. Above all, God wants you to take time for Him.

—DAVID EGNER

FOLLOW THE COMPASS

How's life? Too busy? Start by keeping track of how you spend your time. Can anything be eliminated? Use that extra time to slow down and spend a little extra time with God.

From the Guidebook: Read Psalm 48

HUNTING: Use a propane lantern rather than a flashlight for tracking a wounded deer at night. Blood shows up better under a lantern than with a flashlight.

95. THE MESSAGE OF SPRING

"For God so loved the world that he gave his one and only Son, that whoever believes in him shall not perish but have eternal life."

JOHN 3:16

By the time April arrives in my part of the world, the drab death-look of winter starts being replaced by the rebirth of spring. As the days grow longer, winter's snow cover recedes. Warm rains fall to earth to hurry the season. Wildflowers poke their petals through the leaf-covered forest floor, and tree buds explode—giving way to their newborn leaves. Songbirds' choruses resonate throughout the meadows with songs of hope. From valley floor to ridge tops the wild turkey's booming gobbles proclaim for all to hear. Spring has arrived!

In so many ways spring is the beginning of a journey—spring to summer, summer to autumn, and then autumn's transition to the dead of winter. These seasonal shifts vividly show us the cycle of life.

Creation is meant to lead us to God and of all the seasons, spring does it best. It not only manifests God's miraculous wonders, it also offers hope. This season not only shows us how nature is reborn but it also provides a visual picture of what resurrection is all about. Our springtime rebirth takes

FAST FACT:

Spring begins on the vernal equinox, when day and night are nearly the same length (equinox means "equal night"). Easter falls on the first Sunday after the first full moon after the vernal equinox.

place when we acknowledge that we are sinners and that God loved us so much that He sent His son to earth to die for us. And by asking Jesus to forgive us of our sins and be Lord of our life, for the rest of our life we gain the assurance that we will spend eternity with Him in heaven.

—CHARLES ALSHEIMER

FOLLOW THE COMPASS

Have you acknowledged the truth that you are a sinner who needs a Savior? Many refuse to believe this truth and therefore forfeit their opportunity for eternal joy.

From the Guidebook: Read Romans 3:21–26.

HUNTING: One of the most important items on a bow is the string. Without the string, the bow can't be shot. To lengthen the life of a bowstring and make sure it doesn't break in the field, wax it regularly. A tube of wax costs a few dollars and keeps an expensive bowstring going for several hunting seasons.

96. THE FROG'S "BLACKBOARD"

"Turn my eyes away from worthless things;
preserve my life according to your word."

PSALM 119:37

As a young boy, one of my favorite pastimes was hunting frogs along the banks of a pond near our home. While stalking those green leapers, I was unaware of their unique visual powers that enabled them to elude me so easily. Later I learned that the frog's optical field of perception is like a blackboard wiped clean, and that the only images it receives are objects that directly concern him—such as his natural enemies or the food he needs for survival. Therefore these amphibious little creatures are never distracted by unimportant things but are aware only of essentials and whatever may be dangerous to them.

FAST FACT:

Frogs have vision that allows them to see nearly in a 360-degree manner around them. They need this because their necks aren't very flexible.

Although such restricted eyesight would result in an unimaginable handicap to man, nevertheless a spiritual lesson can be learned from the frog's "blackboard." In the Christian life we frequently become preoccupied with the vain things of the world. We allow our lives to become so cluttered with materialistic and insignificant concerns that we lose perspective of the "things that endure." In our text the psalmist asks God for help in fixing his attention on what is good and lasting.

Solomon also reminds us that the words of the Lord should not depart from our eyes, but be kept in our hearts always (Proverbs 4:21). If we heed his admiration, our field of vision will be wiped clean of unnecessary things, and we will see clearly what God wants us to do.

Have you become distracted by sin so that you can no longer discern what is really important? Then take a lesson from the frog's "blackboard" and center your gaze upon Christ and His will for your life!

—MART DE HAAN

FOLLOW THE COMPASS

Is there anything that is clogging up your vision of God—something that makes it hard for you to see God working in your life? What can you do to change that?

From the Guidebook: Read Psalm 119:33–40.

FISHING: A light rain can help your fishing success because it prevents the fish from seeing through the surface to detect you or your fishing gear.

97. RUSTY GUN

"Do not store up for yourselves treasures on earth, where moth and rust destroy, and where thieves break in and steal. But store up for yourselves treasurers in heaven."

MATTHEW 6:19–21

Hunters need to take care of their guns, or they can easily rust. Recently, I hunted wild turkeys early in the morning. Shortly after it started getting light, rain began to fall. I knew there were turkeys near me, including one large tom, so I stuck it out. But that morning the turkeys weren't cooperative, so I eventually packed up and left. When I got to the car, I wiped off my gun and put it in my case.

FAST FACT:
The best way to avoid "rust prints" on your gun is to wipe it down with a silicon cloth.

When I got home, I had a few things that had to be done right away, so it was a couple of hours before I took my gun out of the case to clean it. Even though I had left it for just a short time, I noticed that light rust was beginning to form on some areas.

The Bible tells us not to store up treasures on earth but instead to lay up for ourselves treasures in heaven. God is not saying that we earn our salvation by what we do; that comes totally by grace with faith in Jesus Christ. On the other hand, God doesn't want us to miss out on rewards in heaven.

—MAURY DE YOUNG

FOLLOW THE COMPASS

Think of it this way: Do you invest as much in God's kingdom as you spend on hunting/fishing/outdoor equipment in a year? Or do you have matching time in an eternal investment with the vacations you take each year?

From the Guidebook: Read I Timothy 6:17 and John 10:10.

HUNTING: Placing a small piece of electrical tape over the tip of a gun barrel can keep dirt, ice, and debris out of the end of an open barrel. Debris and dirt can rob guns of accuracy or cause a barrel to mushroom upon firing, which can cause serious injuries. The tape is inexpensive insurance.

98. WATCHA FISHIN' FOR?

On Point:
Seeking God's kingdom first

"But seek first his kingdom and his righteousness, and all these things will be given to you as well."

MATTHEW 6:33

Fishing is no longer dropping a line into the creek to snag a bluegill. It is very big business. At least for tournament fishermen.

Elite Series angler Kevin Short said, "This is big-time competition among big-time competitors." In 2006 the most elite anglers in the world were being awarded nearly $7.5 million for winning tournaments. With the plethora of fishing tournaments today, anglers have the opportunity to cash in on more than $11 million. Denny Brauer, the first angler featured on the Wheaties cereal box, said, "Sure, the entry fees are high, but the upside is huge, and I am just tickled to have the opportunity to fish for all that money. I feel like I can make a lot of money next year."

FAST FACT:
Recent Elite Series entry fees have been valued at $55,000.

What once was a leisurely Sunday afternoon activity has now become a major competitive sport populated with keenly focused and highly skilled professional fishermen. What are they really after? What drives them, motivates them to catch more little green fish than the next guy? Is it the thrill of competition? Big green money? A chance at fame?

What about you—what motivates you? Is there something in your life that drives you? Jesus simply and boldly tells us, "But seek first his kingdom and his righteousness, and all these things will be given to you as well" (Matthew 6:33). I challenge you to be driven by God and His reign—in other words, to know what you are "after": the work of the kingdom of God.

—MOLLY RAMSEYER

FOLLOW THE COMPASS

If you were to list the top three things you are after in this life, what would they be?

From the Guidebook: Read Matthew 6:19–34. What is Jesus trying to teach in these verses? What does that mean for the things you possess in your life?

FISHING: Not all fishing hooks are created equal. Inexpensive hooks get dull quicker and bend easier than high-quality hooks. Paying a couple extra dollars for good hooks could result in a hook that is tough as nails and as sharp as a razor blade. These two qualities will put more fish in the cooler.

99. PERSEVERANCE

"I can do everything through him who gives me strength."
PHILIPPIANS 4:13

Baseball is an incredible game that can teach lessons about life. It's a game about failure because even a .300 hitter fails 70 percent of the time. To succeed in baseball requires more than talent; it requires perseverance to keep going up to bat when failure is the rule of the day.

From Little League through college I played organized baseball. The lessons I learned from my failures on the diamond helped mold the way I've approached my journey as an outdoor writer and nature photographer. You see, like baseball, nature photography and hunting are about failure because more times than not the animal you are pursuing fails to cooperate. In many cases it takes numerous attempts to get just the right photo or be in position to harvest an animal.

FAST FACT:
Charles Alsheimer coached baseball for many years after his own playing career ended.

Our walk with God also requires us to persevere, because we all stray from God's will from time to time. No matter how hard we try we are all sinners. Like the batter who takes his eye off the ball and strikes out, we too stumble when we take our eyes off of God.

The only way to have a strong walk with the Lord is to persevere by reading the Bible, learning the Scriptures, spending time alone with God in prayer, and trusting and obeying Him.

—CHARLES ALSHEIMER

FOLLOW THE COMPASS

What is your greatest "perseverance" challenge in your walk
with God? Is it sticking with a routine of Bible reading and
prayer? Is there a temptation that keeps after you?

From the Guidebook: Read Philippians 4:12–14.

HUNTING: Wash your hunting clothes with scent eliminator
soap and store them in a dry plastic bag.

100. DON'T GET GREEDY

On Point:
Figuring out what is really important

"A man's life does not consist in the abundance of his possessions."

Luke 12:15

Philip Parham tells the story of a rich industrialist who was disturbed to find a fisherman sitting lazily beside his boat. "Why aren't you out there fishing?" he asked.

"Because I've caught enough fish for today," said the fisherman.

"Why don't you catch more fish than you need?" the rich man asked.

"What would I do with them?"

"You could earn more money," came the impatient reply, "and buy a better boat so you could go deeper and catch more fish. You could purchase nylon nets, catch even more fish, and make more money. Soon you'd have a fleet of boats and be rich like me."

The fisherman asked, "Then what would I do?"

"You could sit down and enjoy life," said the industrialist.

"What do you think I'm doing now?" the fisherman replied as he looked placidly out to sea.

FAST FACT:

Looking for a fishing job that can earn you a boatload of money? Try Alaska. People working on salmon fishing boats can make as much as $40,000 in three months.

We chuckle. Yet that story highlights an important truth. If we live only to accumulate material wealth, we'll never get enough. We'll work more and more frantically—until we collapse!

Been working all the time? Refusing to take vacations? Life is more than possessions. Learn to trust more fully in the God who has given us all things to enjoy.

—DAVID EGNER

FOLLOW THE COMPASS

What is your goal in life? Accumulate stuff? Or build up treasures in heaven? Sure it's important to make a living, but should you vow to put God's priorities before your own?

From the Guidebook: Read Luke 12:13–21.

FISHING: If you are practicing catch and release, don't keep the fish out of the water longer than you can hold your own breath.

KEY VERSE LIST

Verse	Article Number	Title
Genesis 27:2	20	Don't Wait Too Long!
Exodus 20:3	19	Ice Fishing
Deuteronomy 31:6	79	Are You on the Right Path?
Joshua 23:14	14	A Fishing Finality!
I Samuel 12:24	55	The Gift
I Samuel 17:48–49	33	Face Your Giants
I Samuel 24:10	16	The Eyes of Compassion
Nehemiah 4:6	37	Having a Mind to Work
Job 5:7	13	Trouble Is Coming
Job 39:6	80	The Lesson of the Osprey
Psalm 1:2	66	Always on Target
Psalm 6:2, 4	48	Too Weak to Fight?
Psalm 23:4	8	Here Today, Gone Tomorrow
Psalm 37:4	40	Wishes and Hopes
Psalm 48:9	94	Take Time
Psalm 46:10	65	Creation Deficit Disorder
Psalm 51:12	75	When Doubts Arise—Look Up!
Psalm 42:5	69	Discouraged?
Psalm 81:13	89	The Buzzing of the Flies
Psalm 119:37	96	The Frog's "Blackboard"
Psalm 119:165	15	Loss of Direction
Psalm 139:24	7	Check the Compass
Psalm 143:9	34	Run for Cover
Psalm 148:3	82	Camping for Praise
Proverbs 3:5	92	A Trusty Brittany
Proverbs 3:6	54	Aim at the Target
Proverbs 4:23	38	Aim for the Heart
Proverbs 22:6	32	Love is Spelled T-I-M-E
Isaiah 26:3	58	Keep Focused

DEVOTIONAL WRITERS

Brief biographical notes about the writers whose articles appear in the Power Up! *Outdoorsman's edition. Some of these articles first appeared in* Our Daily Bread, *some appeared in* Power Up!, *and some were written especially for this book.*

CHARLES ALSHEIMER A renowned outdoors photographer, Charlie has earned the highest respect from his industry. One deer-hunting magazine named him one of its Top 5 inspirational people of the 20th century. His stories and his sincerity make him a successful writer and speaker on the subject of the outdoors. www.charliealsheimer.com

HENRY BOSCH In 1956, while working at Radio Bible Class, Henry Bosch came up with the idea for *Our Daily Bread.* He was the first editor of that publication.

DAVE BRANON For 18 years, Dave was managing editor of *Sports Spectrum* magazine. Currently, he is an editor for Discovery House and Our Daily Bread Ministries. He is a regular contributing writer for *Our Daily Bread.* Over the years, he has written a number of sports-related books for a variety of publishers.

TRACY BREEN By overcoming cerebral palsy and through his strong faith, Tracy has built a career as an outdoors writer. He hunts and fishes across North America, opening up many doors for his writing and speaking ministry. www.tracybreen.com

DAN DEAL After working as a radio producer and occasional host of *Sports Spectrum* radio at Our Daily Bread Ministries for several years, Deal left to work on the staff of Ada Bible Church in Ada, Michigan, as director of small group training and resources.

DENNIS DEHAAN For many years, Dennis was managing editor of *Our Daily Bread*. A former pastor, he worked at Our Daily Bread Ministries from 1973 until 1995.

MART DEHAAN Mart is senior content editor for Our Daily Bread Ministries. His grandfather, Dr. M. R. DeHaan, founded Radio Bible Class (now Our Daily Bread Ministries) in 1938. Mart has written several books, including *Been Thinking About*, a publication of Discovery House.

M. R. DEHAAN In 1938, Dr. M. R. DeHaan began broadcasting a radio program that represented the beginning of this ministry. The author of a number of books, Dr. DeHaan was an avid outdoorsman.

RICHARD DEHAAN The son of ministry founder Dr. M. R. DeHaan, Richard was president of the ministry for 20 years. He was the founder of the television program *Day of Discovery*, which has been on the air for more than 40 years.

MAURY DE YOUNG A former pastor, Maury is the executive director of Sportspersons Ministries International. This organization attempts to use hunting and fishing to interest men and women in the gospel of Jesus Christ through dinners, outings, and seminars connected with the outdoors. www.spi-int.org

DAVID EGNER A longtime editor and writer at Our Daily Bread Ministries, as well as a popular college professor at Cornerstone University, Egner loves anything outdoors. Golf is on that list of favorites, as is fishing and hunting at his cabin in Michigan's Upper Peninsula.

VERNON GROUNDS A former board member for Our Daily Bread Ministries, Dr. Grounds most recently was chancellor of Denver Seminary. He wrote many books and was a contributing writer for *Our Daily Bread*.

ERIC JONES A former staff member for *Sports Spectrum* magazine, Eric wrote a number of devotional articles for the *Power Up!* devotional. His dad, Bobby, is a former NBA player for the Philadelphia 76ers.

JEFF OLSON When he has to put down his fishing gear or his hunting rifle and come inside, Jeff can be coaxed back to his desk at Our Daily Bread Ministries, where he is a biblical counselor. Olson has written several booklets for the Discovery Series Bible studies. Besides his work with Our Daily Bread Ministries, Olson has a private counseling practice.

MOLLY RAMSEYER As a college student, Molly worked with *Sports Spectrum* magazine as an intern. She did such a good job she was later offered the chance to write for the magazine as a freelancer. After college, she began working with Youth for Christ. Currently, she is national director of camping for Youth for Christ. She lives in Englewood, Colorado, with her family.

ROXANNE ROBBINS After hobnobbing with the influential and famous in Washington, D. C., for several years in positions relating to public relations, Roxanne left it all behind to go to Uganda to live among kids with nothing. A longtime writer for *Sports Spectrum*, she knows athletes up-close and personal, but she has discovered the importance of the oft-neglected little guys and girls who cherish someone who cares for them.

HADDON ROBINSON A former seminary president, Dr. Robinson teaches at Gordon-Conwell Theological Seminary. He formerly wrote for *Our Daily Bread* and participated in a radio discussion program called *Discover the Word*.

DAVID ROPER A prolific writer, Roper has written several books for men—urging them to live for God—including *A Man to Match the Mountain* and *The Strength of a Man* for Discovery House. He and his wife live in Idaho, which offers him a great opportunity to engage in his favorite recreation: fly-fishing.

HERB VANDER LUGT For a long time, Herb was one of the most popular writers at Our Daily Bread Ministries. His clear understanding of theology and life helped him as he wrote for *Our Daily Bread* and for several Discovery Series booklets. A pastor and an avid baseball fan, Herb loved to regale his listeners with stories of his youth as a catcher and as a fan who loved going to Tiger Stadium to see greats like Hank Greenberg play. He continued to work at the ministry until his death in 2006.

PAUL VAN GORDER A former Bible teacher for Our Daily Bread Ministry radio and television, Paul wrote for *Our Daily Bread* for many years.

NOTE TO THE READER

The publisher invites you to share your response to the message of this book by writing Discovery House, P.O. Box 3566, Grand Rapids, MI 49501, U.S.A. For information about other Discovery House books, music, or DVDs, contact us at the same address or call 1-800-653-8333. Find us on the Internet at dhp.org or send e-mail to books@dhp.org.